Financial Wisdom for Physicians

Running a Successful Practice,
Managing Your Personal Finances,
and Investing for Success

by

Joseph S. Zasa

Contents

Introduction	3
Forward	7
Preface	11
Chapter 1 - You are who you are, not what you do - Building Your Tribe Part I	15
Chapter 2 - Building your Practice	24
Chapter 3 - Medical Billing Economics/How Physicians Bill & Collect and Why this is Important	45
Chapter 4 - Understanding Financial Statements	55
Chapter 5 - Creating and Interacting with your Tribe: Part II	65
Chapter 6 - Foundations of Personal Finance	85
Chapter 7 - Personal Finance	91
Chapter 8 - Investing and Retirement Planning	127
Chapter 9 - Portfolio Construction	149
Chapter 10 - The Role of Alternative Investments & Evaluating Ancillary Deals	159
Conclusion	167
About the Author	169
Appendix I - Should We Be Tactical?	170
Appendix II - An Interview with Robin Wigglesworth about Index Funds	176
Appendix III - A Primer on Legal Issues	188
Appendix IV - Recommended Reading	204
Appendix V - Summary of the Core Concepts	206
Acknowledgements	207

Introduction

This book provides tools to acquire financial and business literacy. It is written for medical students, health administration students, and physicians in practice. My experience teaching future healthcare professionals and practicing physicians is that all have a real desire to learn these skills because they have not been taught how to negotiate their salary or partnership agreements, how to manage money, how to invest, how to make key purchases, how to manage debt and how to be savvy making financial and life decisions.

I have a somewhat unique background and it is a contributing factor for this book. I grew up wanting to be an investment banker. My undergraduate degree is in Economics, the study of allocating resources aimed at needs and wants. Economics and the related curriculum focus on finance, accounting, monetary policy, and how money flows through our commercial system. It provides a fabulous theoretical grounding in business. After graduating college, I went to law school instead of business school because law school best afforded me the skills to be a businessman. Law school for me was like an engineering degree for business - it was practical and taught me how taxes work, corporations are formed and operate, the role of directors, how securities are registered and sold, and how businesses are purchased and valued. In sum, college taught me conceptually about money, and law school taught me critical thinking and gave me the tools necessary to consummate deals. It also taught me how to protect myself in the business world.

For the last thirty years, I have been the CEO of a healthcare company specializing in developing and managing surgery centers. I estimate that we have worked with over 1,000 physicians as partners in the surgery centers that we manage. The relationships developed over time and the myriad of experiences were a major motivation for writing this book.

INTRODUCTION

In 2016, I was asked to teach a course at the University of Alabama Birmingham School of Health Professions focusing on starting and operating a healthcare business. I still teach this course. I also teach at the University of Alabama Birmingham Heersink School of Medicine a course entitled "Business Concepts and Personal Finance for Physicians." Each year the students ask me about personal finances, investments, taxes, wills and trusts, and other concepts. It became clear to me that there is a real gap in education regarding personal finance and a real desire to learn these concepts. Teaching is a calling, and my students require a much-needed grounding in how to choose a job, questions to ask, key tenets to discern making career decisions, investment theory, how markets work, how to manage personal finances, how to manage debt, how to invest, how to run a business and how to protect yourself from charlatans. They are the reason this book was written.

It is my steadfast hope that this book will be a contribution to the subject of financial literacy. The goal is for you to use this book to free yourself of financial worry: to learn how to invest, not spend everything you make, not be controlled by debt, not be taken advantage of by unscrupulous advisors, and free yourself to take care of your patients and pursue your life goals. Over the years, I have learned key lessons and I hope to convey those lessons to you through this book.

I hope you enjoy this book as much as I did in writing it.

— Joe Zasa
December 18, 2021
Shoal Creek, Alabama

Forward

Almost 40 years ago, fresh out of my post residency fellowship training, I accepted a position in the Orthopaedic group I still work with (albeit, now under a new corporate owner). I accepted the job based on the community standing of the group members, clinical opportunities, a common goal and vision by the physicians and general sense of "well-being" across the practice. Note that I have not mentioned ANY financial components associated with this decision. With zero fiscal or practice management instruction during my medical training and business sense limited to a general understanding of CPT and ICD codes (and that they were "important"), the first decades of a (mostly) financially successful medical practice may best viewed as mix of dumb luck, no irretrievably bad business decisions and learning on the fly.

I wish I had this book then!

One thing our group realized was that the direction of operative care was evolving to a non hospital based setting. Taking the plunge to build and operate a free-standing Ambulatory Surgery Center, we were smart enough to know what we wanted but also that we did not how to get there – enter Joe Zasa. We did our due diligence, found the person who best aligned with our vision, who could advise and direct us through the process, and was willing to take the same risks as we would take to build something new, better and nurture it so it would grow and succeeded, AKA Joe Z.

Twenty years later, I can say that Joe has been a business associate, mentor, educator, sounding board, cheerleader, naysayer/voice of reason when needed and navigator through the challenges of regulatory change, demographic shifts, evolving payment models, changes in practice profile and the new paradigm of health care during Covid.

FOREWARD

This book is an essential primer for fiscal competence. While primarily directed at health care providers, the information provided is a valuable resource for anyone who wants a long term plan for sound financial decisions and success.

The organization is straightforward, chapters constructed in a well defined and cohesive manner that allows them to be read as part of the whole concept or as stand alone, and the information from Mr. Zasa and the supporting contributors provides real world perspectives that make complicated financial, business model and legal topics "digestible".

Joe has put together a valuable accumulation of ideas, theories, practical advice, and strategies that can be used across the breadth of one's medical (and business) career. It is not just information; it is a strategy for sound fiscal management and security. Medicine is a business, and this should be viewed an essential component of medical education and as a long-term resource.

As I stated earlier, I wish this book had existed when I began my medical practice. After several read throughs of the book, I am still finding information and fiscal direction that I will be using through the waning phase of my medical career and beyond. Read it in good (financial) health.

Thanks Joe.

TK Miller, MD is the Vice Chairman and Section Chief of Sports Medicine for the Department of Orthopaedic Surgery at Carilion Clinic and holds an academic appointment as Professor in the Department of Orthopaedic Surgery at the Virginia Tech Carilion School of Medicine.

He serves as the Medical Director of the Roanoke Ambulatory Surgery Center in Roanoke Virginia.

Preface

We are in the healthcare business. This presents a dichotomy because the goal of a business is to maximize profit, and the directive for the healthcare practitioner is to heal patients. An extreme view on either side of this statement is at best, short-sighted. At worst, it shows ignorance. I firmly believe that profit and quality of care are not mutually exclusive and the healthcare practitioner who is well versed in both medicine and business, can marry both philosophies together to become a more effective physician and improve the patient experience.

You may have heard the saying "Doctors aren't good businessmen." Maybe, but my experience is that most businessmen <u>are not good businessmen</u>. Therefore, the goal of this book is to highlight key skills necessary for a new or experienced physician so that you are versed in core financial and business concepts and have the tools necessary to build a successful practice, manage your finances, and build wealth.

The emphasis of this book is focused on:

- The Secret to Being a Successful Physician: Understanding how to connect and interact with those who will assist you and make you successful: patients, colleagues, referring physicians, staff, and administration.

- How to Choose a Practice: questions and steps needed to assess whether you will be employed or join a private practice, how to assess a practice, how to negotiate your compensation, how to assess partnership opportunities, and negotiate partnership or employment agreements.

- How to Run a Profitable and Effective Practice: Understanding the physician revenue cycle process: authorizations, verifications, billing, coding, collecting, and contracting with payers and learning how to maximize efficiencies within those systematic functions. Understanding how money flows through the system and your role in that system, including the dichotomy between patient care and profit.

- Building a *Tribe*: Understanding the importance of building a core team of advisors that protect your interests such as lawyers, accountants, bankers, and consultants, and learning how to choose those members of your tribe.

- Understanding Basic Healthcare Legal Principles: Anti-Kickback, Stark and other laws physicians must understand.

- Managing Your Personal Finances: How to manage debt, how to purchase a home, how to purchase a car, key steps to controlling personal expenses, and how to reduce stress by making money work for you instead of you working for money.

- Investing for Success: Having a fundamental understanding of basic investing concepts, understanding how markets work, stocks, bonds, real estate, and alternative investments; and finally,

- Fundamental Portfolio Construction: Concepts and key tenets to achieve wealth.

Importantly, the concepts learned and applied will protect you from financial predators and will give you the basics so you can establish yourself on solid financial ground and have the time to enjoy your life's ambitions.

Chapter 1
You are who you are, not what you do

You may be surprised that this book doesn't start with reading financial statements or some esoteric concept such as the difference between cash and accrual accounting. Rather, this book starts with people. Specifically, how you handle yourself and the people in your world.

The famous football coach Lou Holtz says, "Ego stands for Edging Greatness Out". The core principle is: **Don't be a jerk.** You don't know everything. While you do have to prove yourself, and you will through your skills developed in medical school and residency, you will also do it through the acquired skill of *emotional intelligence* – how you interact with people.

Emotional intelligence is the capacity to be aware of, control, and express one's emotions, and to handle interpersonal relationships judiciously and empathetically. It is understanding the concept of division of labor and strategically building a team or tribe of others who can assist you with differing skills.

Chapter 1 - You are who you are, not what you do.

A couple of stories to highlight this concept:

In 1992, I graduated law school, passed the Virginia Bar, and started acquiring surgery centers on behalf of my company. I thought I knew it all until an older nurse took me under her wing, explained to me that "I knew nothing" and showed me how surgery centers truly work. She strongly emphasized winning over the staff and becoming part of the organization rather than acting like the organization works for you. She emphasized what we now call *servant leadership* in which the **goal of the leader is to serve**. ... A servant-leader shares power, puts the needs of the employees first, and helps people develop and perform as highly as possible. Instead of the people working to serve the leader, the leader exists to serve the people.

Being trained by someone in the field was a gift because it helped me understand how an organization works, how to take care of the people in your organization, work for them and pursue a common goal. Reta Turner was willing to mentor me and she changed my career path from being a "suit who did deals" to a manager who does his best to show respect for the people in our firm by listening and leading by example. My company, ASD Management, is a very successful firm, and it would not have happened if I had not learned this lesson. Fortunately for me, Reta and I still speak, and she still advises me to this day even after retiring at 85 from a 20+ year career with us.

When Bear Bryant came back to Alabama in 1960 as head coach, his first recruiting trip was to a small town in Alabama. He stopped at a roadside restaurant and asked for directions after introducing himself and then decided to stay for lunch. The owner told him that he probably would not like the food because it was chitlins (pig intestines) and greens. Bryant told him he grew up on that food and later told the owner how much he enjoyed meeting him and how much he enjoyed his cooking. The owner asked Coach Bryant for an autographed picture and Bryant explained that he was newly hired, didn't even have business cards much less photos, but if the owner would write down the address, Bryant would send him a signed photo. Thirty years later, Alabama was recruiting a star football

Chapter 1 - You are who you are, not what you do.

prospect, but he told the Bear that he made up his mind and was committed to Auburn (Alabama's biggest rival) and Auburn was his "dream" school. The next day, the same recruit called Coach Bryant and asked if the offer was still open to play at Alabama. Coach Bryant said "yes" but was wondering why the recruit changed his mind. The recruit said that his grandfather had met Bryant years ago and the Coach had indeed sent the signed picture that still hangs up in the restaurant today. The recruit said he had no choice because his grandfather insisted that he play for Bear Bryant since "the Bear kept his promise" and forged a relationship that day.

Bottom Line: It costs nothing to be nice.

One of the ways we evaluate people is to see how they treat those who are subordinate to them. It is a key barometer. It is suggested that you do the same.

Due to your medical degree and social standing, you will be in a position of power. Learning how to use that power is critical to your long-term success. Don't be seduced by flattery or believe that you are the smartest person in the room. No matter whom you meet, someone is superior to you in some way, and you can learn from them. Arrogance and ignorance are a recipe for disaster. Use your power and social standing to help others and you will be happier.

> ## Thus, the first lesson is:
> ## It's all about People.

The first thing to understand with people is their agenda. Everyone has an agenda and that is neither good nor bad. Put yourself in the other person's shoes and understand their motivation. Then, build alliances with them. These are your strategic partners and focus on them because they help you fulfill your agenda. There is a saying, "the more people I like, the happier I am." Be a light for everyone, even those who do not appear to be needed, and you will be surprised.

Chapter 1 - You are who you are, not what you do.

Building your Internal Tribe: Part I

Your *Internal Tribe* is the group of people you interact with daily. If you effectively build and continually nurture these relationships in a complimentary (not one-sided or selfish) way, your Internal Tribe will protect you and permit you to thrive. This is analogous to wolves who hunt as a group because they are more successful as a unit rather than alone, it perpetuates the pack and furthers the common interest of the pack.

The players in your Internal Tribe:

- **Staff** – understand that your staff supports you and interacts with patients throughout your practice. *You must take care of them – you must win them over.* They must believe that you care about them and will do what is best for the practice to make it successful and strong. This gives them financial and emotional security. Bonuses based on the performance of the practice are a key component, but more importantly, is managing them with kindness, fairness, and giving them a sense of security that you care about them and are a leader they want to follow. In turn, this will trickle down from the top, create a positive culture and be attractive to your patients, colleagues, and referral base. A happy office is the foundation of a successful practice.

- **Staff Part II** – the staff at the hospital including not just the nurses, and techs, but the secretaries and assistants are just as important. Why? They all talk amongst themselves, and your reputation is built through these people. Connect with them, be nice to them, remember their names, ask them about themselves, but do it genuinely. A great and sage saying: "the more people I like, the happier I am."

- **Administrator of your Practice** – your practice administrator runs your practice and implements a positive and welcoming culture for your patients, their families, the staff, and referring physicians. The Administrator must manage your practice within reasonable MGMA financial benchmarks, manage the employees and coordinate with you and your partners on areas related to the practice. A sign of bad management is staff turnover, but also be cognizant of staff gossip and undermining. There must be a balance between micro-managing and empowering. The check and balance on your administrator is your CPA for internal controls, and your business advisor to benchmark financial performance and ensure that the practice plan is being followed.

- **Referral Base and Colleagues** – connect with them regularly, ask what you can do for them, be timely with your follow-up on patients, and do what you say. Obviously, you must establish a relationship with them and highlight your competence. As importantly, is understanding their motivations and doing your best to help them solve their problems.

- **Patients** – your interaction with your patients is what you do – take care of your patients. However, they are also part of your Tribe. They talk, refer friends and acquaintances. Most importantly, they interact with you and are part of your "family."

- **Administration** – you will interact with hospital administration and administration within your office. These are two very different groups. We discussed your practice administrator above as a critical and essential part of your tribe. Additionally, hospital administrators can be a strategic ally. It is important to understand their motivation and they are evaluated by quality and profit measures. At the end of the day, they want you to refer to their hospital. They will assist you economically through guarantees etc. but it still comes back to your loyalty to their health system. If you understand this and try to connect with them, they will be receptive since many physicians are in an adversarial relationship with them. They have a tough job because everyone in the organization presents problems for them to fix. Go to them with solutions based on your agenda that work for both of you. They will be extremely receptive because you are the only one providing a solution instead of lighting a fire and asking them to put it out. Put another way, you attract more flies with honey than vinegar so build a relationship, explain what you need to make both of you successful, and ask for their assistance.

The essential tool that allows you to understand and interact with people is emotional intelligence. Emotional intelligence begets power and the ability to control your agenda. The components are:

1. Self-awareness
2. Self-regulation
3. Motivation
4. Empathy
5. Social Skills

Be the most mature person in the room. Power and influence flow to the most mature person in the room. Work towards mutually beneficial outcomes. Emotional intelligence is a main differentiator between those who are successful and those who are not. How do you acquire and exercise Emotional Intelligence?

- Listen - People want to feel included and heard. Encourage them to talk about themselves. People want to be understood. Don't be formulating your response while others are speaking. Rather, really listen to them and try to understand them. They will listen to you, and you will build lasting relationships.

- Create a Team – To lead is to serve, and to serve is to care. If you want to lead an organization that lasts, create a tribe, enable and support it as the leader. A tribe has its own culture. Make sure that the culture focuses on patient care, safety, and measured success standards.

Chapter 1 - You are who you are, not what you do.

- Build Alliances – The key is alignment of incentives. Ally with your colleagues and partners, referral base, administration, and staff. Talk in terms of other person's interests and show you are genuinely interested in them.

- Create a culture in your office that pursues excellence in patient care and achieves "buy-in" amongst your staff.

- Take care of your referring physicians. Listen to them, communicate with them, make them look good.

- Remember Names – it's hard but it goes a long way.

- Be a Leader - lead by example. Show up on time, do what you say, admit when you are wrong, listen, be a light for others and spread kindness.

- Smile and Make the Other Person Feel Important and be Sincere about it.

CONCEPT 1: *How you deal with people (Patients, Colleagues, Staff, Spouse, Family) will have more to do with your long-term success than your medical skills.* You must have both, but thousands are just as smart, and have the essential skills. Note that nothing about billing or finances was just discussed because they are the secondary lessons. Acquiring emotional intelligence and effectively interacting/connecting with people are the initial building blocks to success in business.

Chapter II
Building your Practice

Let's work in chronological order after medical school graduation and residency.

Should you be Employed or go into Private Practice?

There is no right or wrong choice. Determining where you want to live is a primary and important personal choice. Is it a locale that fits you culturally? Can you see yourself living in that locale long term? Certainly, the decision should be made based on factors unique to each individual. Healthcare is a local business and the market you choose will play a large part in determining the choice between private practice and employment.

Before we address market conditions, there is data published that may be instructive regarding employed versus private practice.

First, according to the American Medical Association, the percentage of doctors with an ownership stake in their practice declined to 47 percent in 2016. As I write this at the end of 2021, my guess is that trend is continuing. Certainly, there is a trend toward being employed, and in fact, the vast majority of the students from my last medical school class will initially be employed. The same study showed that younger physicians are much more likely to be employed than older physicians.

Second, there seems to be no correlation in job satisfaction between employed and independent physicians according to a 2016 study published by Medscape.

Third, based on my research, private practice physicians do not necessarily make more money than employed physicians. There is actually very little discrepancy in income based on the reports reviewed.

The advantages typically cited for employment are:

1. Job security – a physician signs a contract for a specified period and renegotiates, typically, every three years.

2. Simplicity – built-in operational systems and no need to build a practice (hire a manager, staff, etc.) or buy into an existing practice. Many physicians do not feel prepared to start a practice on their own with the related startup costs especially considering many have large medical school debt.

3. Established and Predictable Referral Base – typically, employed physicians are a conglomerate of primary care and specialties creating a network of internal referrals.

4. Lifestyle – you are an employee and not the owner of the business responsible for all aspects of the practice. Flexibility with hours is a key cited advantage of employment. You can work your shift and then go home.

5. Managed Care Contracting – payer agreements are pre-negotiated typically through employment relationship affiliation.

Conversely, the appeal of private practice typically is:

1. Independence – the ability to control one's time and career and not be dependent on a bureaucratic infrastructure.

2. Autonomy of Practice – the ability to spend as much time as required with patients without productivity quotas.

3. Job Security – your job security is a function of your success as a physician treating patients and building a referral network. You are not a cog in the machine but rather a colleague with partners.

4. Greater Income Potential – while the studies cited above show that physicians employed make as much as those in private practice, it is undeniable that income is unlimited if you are self-employed; whereas employed physicians have productivity bonuses and base salaries that are limited.

My view is mixed on this. For physicians with low risk tolerance and/or high debt, the employment model may be a good choice. However, I do believe that some of the data is misleading. For example, the idea that being employed creates job security is problematic at best because most employment agreements have a 90-day without cause termination provision. In any type of employment relationship, you are dependent on one source for your income (your boss); whereas, in a private practice you have multiple income pipelines (your patients). In addition, once the initial contract is finished and it is time to sign again, your employer has all the leverage because you can be replaced with a younger physician at a lower salary since you have no patient base and are reliant on their referral network. Similarly, high job satisfaction with employed physicians may be a function of those who want a lifestyle job. Put another way, "water finds its own level" and those who gravitate to employed relationships tend to be happier in those relationships whereas more entrepreneurial physicians seem to be happier self-employed. Also, the studies that show that there is little income disparity between employed physicians and private practice physicians may be skewed because a successful private practice physician should make more than an employed physician since there are no limits on his or her income. This is similar to small business data that is skewed because the average is not the median. The small businesses that do achieve success make a disproportionate amount of income, so be careful about statistics.

If a physician comes to me and wants to consider private practice, I explain that the price of success is high, but so are the rewards. If that physician is willing to work hard, build a referral network and practice in a geographically desirable and strategic location where he or she can establish their practice or find a practice to join that can grow and build a base that protects from competitors, then creating infrastructure to bill, code and collect, and engaging a team to do managed care contracting can easily be accomplished. Notwithstanding, healthcare is a local business and if all the referring physicians are employed or the payer market is terrible for non-affiliated physicians, then private practice does not make sense. However, if the market is good and/or has room for growth, and the physician has the requisite work ethic and desire to succeed, there are many advantages both economically and emotionally to private practice. Conversely, if the physician has a lower risk tolerance, is in a closed market, or desires a lifestyle job, then being employed is a good option. Finally, a hybrid approach should be considered whereby a physician is initially employed for a few years, then networks in the market establishes herself, and then goes into private practice. Under this scenario, the physician has leverage and can weigh and balance the renewal employment contract with the option of private practice; hence, giving the physician options and leverage during the negotiation that she would not have otherwise.

Chapter 2 - Building your Practice.

Questions to Ask Before Joining a Practice

Once the employment/private practice question is answered, regardless of whether the physician decides to be employed or join a practice, there are several questions to ask:

a) Investigate the reputation of the physicians at the practice. Due diligence is easy today and a quick search for reviews or asking others about the practice and the physicians can easily be done.

b) Can you see yourself working with the partners, particularly the ones closest to your age? Do you like them? It is vital that you listen carefully during your interview and spend as much time with the group as possible. The more time you spend, the better it will be for you because anyone can impress at one meeting, but over time you will get a better feel for them. Ask them questions about how they practice, their goals, the challenges within the practice and the market, how long they want to work, if they feel there is room for growth within the practice, and their expectations of you. The more questions you ask, the better informed you will be to decide regardless of whether this is an employment arrangement or private practice.

c) How long have the partners been at the practice? This is an excellent barometer regarding stability of the group and the practice.

d) Who was the most recent addition to the practice? Are they still there? Can you speak with them?

e) How much turnover have they had with physicians? This is another key indicator. In fact, if you can speak with physicians who have left and can find out their reason for leaving, it will be an indicator. Notwithstanding, some people are not a good fit for the practice or could be chronic malcontents so use their feedback as a piece of the puzzle but not necessarily gospel.

Chapter 2 - Building your Practice.

f) How much turnover has the practice experienced with staff? Staff turnover is a key barometer of management and 10-15% of the employees being replaced in a year is excessive barring external factors. Obviously, COVID-19 has a far-reaching impact so take this into account when assessing turnover.

g) Ask the practice manager if they use third-party accountants to prepare the financials or if they have a third-party audit the practice each year. The concept is that a third-party objective source reviewing the practice is prudent. No audits of the practice or its managers are a red flag.

h) How do the physicians in the practice benchmark financially with similar practices? Similarly, how does the practice benchmark against similar practices? If the manager cannot provide benchmark information, it could be a sign of poor management since these statistics are readily available and the best way to objectively assess a practice.

i) Is the practice profitable? Can you see the financials? This may not be applicable for a group practice employment arrangement but is very important as you contemplate a long-term commitment. See Buying into a Practice below.

j) How much debt does the practice have and is this debt impacting the long-term stability of the practice? Your accountant and advisor can assist with this analysis.

k) Are physicians in the group about to retire? If so, how many? You don't want to be left holding the bag.

l) If joining a practice, when will you be offered partner status? How does this work? Typically, you are required to work for a set period before you will be offered a partnership.

m) If employed, obtain a copy of the employment agreement, and make sure you understand it. It is likely that you will not, so have your business advisor (business consultant See External Tribe below) and/or attorney review all key terms with

Chapter 2 - Building your Practice.

you, so you have a clear understanding of your obligations and those of your employer.

n) Who are the competitors in the market? This is critical to understand before you join a practice because your first years in practice are critical to building your referral and patient base. If you are a surgeon and a key competitor is entering the market and is affiliated with a competing hospital that is buying up primary care practices, this could really impact your ability to build a practice.

o) Does the practice have ancillary businesses? Will you be offered investment in them? For example, surgery centers, imaging centers, lithotripsy partnerships.

p) Does the practice have insurance and will that insurance cover you if you are sued? For example, does the practice have employment practices insurance? There could be a scenario where there may be non-malpractice claims by employees and patients. If you are sued for harassment, the practice should have insurance to cover claims so that you are not required to come out of pocket to defend yourself. The same concepts apply to general liability (slip and fall), business interruption and hazard insurance (fire, storm, water). This is a very important concept and is easily overlooked. The practice must indemnify you (defend you) for basic insurance claims.

q) Does the practice employ managed care contracting services and/or how is payer contracting done? Managed care contracting has a huge impact on your income. The more expertise, the better.

r) Will the practice work with payers to get you credentialed so you can participate in those plans? A lengthy delay will impact your ability to practice adversely.

s) Does the practice cover your malpractice insurance, or will you be responsible for that coverage?

t) Does the practice offer a retirement plan, and does it match your contribution in any way? Does the practice offer other benefits such as a group rate for disability insurance?

u) Does the practice pay for health insurance for you or your family?

v) What is their expectation of you in terms of hours, time off, and billing? What is the call schedule? Again, understanding your role and how you will work within the practice is very important before you join.

CONCEPT 2: You must completely understand all aspects of your employment or partnership arrangement before you commit. In summary, who are you working with and what are the terms of your engagement with the group and expectations from the group?

Negotiating your Compensation

Once you understand the expectations outlined in your employment or partnership agreement, the next key step is how you will be compensated.

Negotiating Salary and Income Guarantees. For those employed as well as those joining a practice, it is typical that there may be some sort of income guarantee initially and then a salary plus bonus thereafter. Another compensation incentive is a school debt reduction arrangement based on tenure. All of these are part of your total compensation.

Therefore, once an offer is received, let's work through how to negotiate your compensation:

1) The first step is to understand all aspects of your compensation offer: salary or draw (payments made to the physician against his or her profit at the end of the year), call pay, ancillary income from the practice from investments such as ambulatory surgery centers, imaging centers, real estate owned by the practice, etc.

2) Next, how did your employer/group derive the offer? A key strategic move is to ask them this question so they can explain the offer.

3) Do not take the first offer. This is a good lesson for all negotiations. Even if you believe that the offer is non-negotiable, it does not hurt to ask for a reasonable amount based on the tactics set forth below because a negotiating tactic is to act as if the offer is "final." Typically, everything is negotiable. This is where your business advisor (business consultant) can assist. Using an advisor as a third party deflects the compensation discussion from you to your "financial advisor."

4) Finally, you (or better your advisor) should use objective compensation benchmarks (your advisor should have them) to justify your counteroffer. Be respectful and show the data from your benchmarks to make a reasonable counter. One last point from my good friend, Tom Clark Esq., who is a successful seasoned negotiator: "He who speaks first loses." Provide a reasonable counteroffer with justified data and then take a deep breath and let them respond. Do not be emotional but rather matter of fact using your objective benchmark data to make your point. They may not like it, but they will respect you. The worst thing that can happen is that they say no since in the extremely unlikely event that they pull the offer, you do not want to work for that group – trust me.

CONCEPT 3: The critical lesson is to *negotiate your compensation* using benchmarks and it is recommended to use a qualified advisor to negotiate on your behalf. Taking the first offer is leaving money on the table in most instances, so be a smart negotiator because you will be working hard and should be paid accordingly and equitably.

Division of Profits

For those joining a private practice or an employed group practice model, the first question to ask is how are profits of the group divided? This may or may not be highlighted in the employment agreement but is more applicable to joining a private practice. The key concern is twofold: 1) Is the income split equitably or are you working and propping up the less productive partners; 2) How can the income allocation be changed in the agreement? For example, after you join, can the partners change your compensation. A common reason that practices break up is over income allocation whereby the most productive partners feel that they should be compensated more than the other partners. It is critical that you understand precisely how you will be compensated and should consult with your advisors prior to joining a practice or signing an employment agreement. Typical private practice physician compensation models include:

1) Employment model with a bonus structure – you are employed and have a base salary plus a bonus based on productivity. The bonus may vary based on your specific performance or the performance of the group collectively. There are too many variations to go into detail on this, so it is suggested that you follow the steps outlined in this chapter and have a clear understanding of your entire compensation package. If you do not understand the bonus or the bonus is entirely subjective and determined without parameters, it is suggested that you renegotiate your arrangement so there are no misunderstandings and objective criteria are used.

2) Independent practice with a shared expense model, and each physician pays their direct expenses – in this model, each physician acts like his or her own solo practitioner and shares expenses with his or her colleagues. Typically, there is an agreement outlining how expenses are shared. There may or not be an income guarantee (that may or may not have to be paid back) if you are a new physician to the market.

3) Partnership Models:

   A. All partners split expenses equally and take an equal salary but have a bonus structure for over-producing physicians above the baseline set.

   B. All partners collect their own rendering collections, split any ancillaries evenly, and all partners pay their direct cost and then split equally certain costs (management fees, office staff, rent, and other general and administrative expenses). Based on experience, this is the most common group practice compensation model.

   C. All partners pay their direct expenses, share common expenses, split ancillary income equally for Medicare, but take their own commercial ancillaries, and keep their own collections.

Buying into a Practice

If a physician is buying into a practice regardless of whether it is at the start of his or her career or after practicing for a few years, there are several key considerations associated with being an owner in a practice. The first determinate for the physician purchaser is to understand what they are purchasing.

Questions to ask:

1) Are you purchasing a percentage ownership in the group or the entire practice? Are there non-compete provisions in your agreement? If so, how long and what is the radius? Typically, two years after you leave the practice and a radius that defines the market is common. Try not to sign a noncompete and this should be part of the negotiation.

2) What is included in the purchase of the practice? For example, does this include real estate or any of the ancillary services? If not, how long is your lease? How is it valued? Make

Chapter 2 - Building your Practice.

sure that the lease is a fair market, and you aren't paying one of your partners or an affiliate above market rates.

3) What assets are included? Typically, a practice has very little in terms of real assets. The accounts receivable and medical equipment are the most common tangible assets other than real estate (the building or land where the practice is located). The real asset is the referral base and patients of the practices and their records.

4) How much debt does the practice have? Are you required to sign on to this debt? If so, is it joint and several or prorata? Joint and several liability is a key concept and is <u>incredibly important</u> to understand because it is probably the most common reason for physician bankruptcy. To illustrate, if you sign a guarantee for debt with others and it is *joint and several*, the bank can come after you for all the debt regardless of your ownership percentage. Note that this will be standard in loan agreements but signing these types of guarantees <u>are not recommended</u>. For example, you and your cousin open a nightclub and sign a banknote for $500,000. You and your cousin are 50/50 partners. When the club your cousin is managing (predictably) fails, if the guarantee is *joint and several*, the bank will come after you for the entire $500,000 even though you only own 50% of the club. They will do this because you are the deep pocket. Conversely, *prorated guarantees* must be negotiated and stated clearly in the loan agreement. In the example above, the prorated guarantee would likely be 1.2 times your percentage ownership or 1.2 x $250,000. The key is that must know what type of guarantee of debt you are signing and have your business advisor assist you in negotiating loan guarantees because they are typically negotiable. Bottom line: Do not sign joint and several guarantees. The other thing to remember is that if you are being asked to assume debt or sign a loan you must know the personal financial condition of the other guarantors, or the company/partnership, and most importantly make sure you can absorb it financially if the note is called.

5) Is the referral base solid, or are the primary care physicians being purchased and expected to be forced to refer elsewhere? You should obtain a breakdown of referral sources by percentage: physician and other provider referrals, referrals from the internet (very important now), from ERs, and other sources that may vary by specialty.

6) Can you buy in over time or do they expect payment for your interest in a lump sum?

There are two traditional models for valuing a practice.

1) A Negotiated Amount; and

2) An Appraised Valuation Approach

A set negotiated amount may vary from $1.00 to whatever the seller believes the practice is worth. The better approach is to engage your advisor and/or accountant to value the practice using recognized methods. One such method is to determine the asset value of the business and subtract the liabilities to arrive at book value or shareholder equity. While this is a recognized method by the Internal Revenue Service, it may undervalue the business because the business value is really a function of the income it produces. Accordingly, a better-recognized method is a discounted cash flow approach. While this sounds esoteric and hard to understand, it is not. The valuation is based on the expected income from the practice over a period and then a percentage rate is assigned that will discount those earnings in future years based on the risk associated. The discount rate is expressed as a percentage and the concept is that a dollar today is worth less than the same dollar in five years as an example. The lower the discount rate, the higher the value of the business because the lower rate will discount the earnings less than a higher rate. For example, a discount rate of 4% recognizes that the practice is stable and an investor investing in the practice would be satisfied with that rate of return due to its stability. Conversely, a high discount rate such as 18% suggests that the practice has more risk and 18% must be used to compensate the investor for the risk. In summary, the discounted cash flow model easily can be run by the accountant for the physician so a reasonable value can be derived for the practice. Negotiating the value is not dissimilar to negotiating compensation by using objective data to derive the value.

Partnership Agreement Considerations

Once the value of the practice is negotiated, your healthcare attorney who is familiar with physician clients buying into practices will work through the purchase agreement and the partnership agreement with you. To expand on what was discussed above, you must clearly understand the partnership agreement terms including:

1) How will you be compensated, and how are profits split? See the above discussion regarding compensation strategies and division of profits.

2) What happens if a non-adverse salient event occurs with you or one of your partners such as death, disability, or retirement? Typically, there is a buyout formula that is set in place using an average of the earnings of the practice historically and then the partner's buyout is paid out over time. Divorce is another event that should be mentioned. Many states are community property states whereby any property in a marriage is split evenly upon divorce. If the partnership agreement is not drafted properly, it could result in a spouse owning a piece of the practice, so make sure that is addressed by having the spouse sign the partnership agreement and certify that they have no rights to the practice upon divorce.

3) What happens if an adverse salient event occurs such as conviction of a felony, fraud, or malfeasance? Under this circumstance, the partner is bought out at a heavily discounted value.

4) Are there non-competition provisions in the agreement? If so, how long and what is the radius? Typically, two years after you leave the practice and a radius that defines the market is standard. Non-competition agreements cut both ways. On the one hand, noncompete agreements provide security so that you know your future partners won't walk away and open another practice down the road and leave you with all the overhead. On the other hand, once you sign a non-compete, if you leave the practice for any reason, you will be restricted from practicing within that market. As discussed above, the radius for a non-compete varies based on the market. For example, a radius in Wyoming could be 100 miles, whereas, in Manhattan, it could be based on neighborhoods. Regardless, there are considerations associated with non-competes and you must clearly understand the pros and cons before signing.

5) How will the practice be governed and managed? If you join a practice and the senior partners make all the decisions, this could be adverse to your interests. The partnership agreement should have rights for minority partners, partners who do not represent the majority of the ownership. For example, can you unilaterally ask for an audit of the practice without the approval of the other partners? It is important to note that much of this has to do with your relationship with your partners and many of the points in this section contemplate what happens if there are philosophical or material differences between the parties.

6) Can the practice enter into agreements with affiliated members? For example, if the building is owned by one of the physicians but not the other partners, we strongly suggest that the agreement calls for the landlord partner to recuse himself from votes or discussions regarding the rent or the real estate, and no agreements are entered with an affiliated partner unless it is independently determined that the service is being provided at fair market value.

Chapter 2 - Building your Practice.

7) Can partners be voted out, and if so, how does this occur, and is it equitable? You must understand how this works, how the practice is valued for a partner who is leaving, and how that partner will be paid.

> CONCEPT 4: Before you buy into a practice, make sure that you understand the key terms of your partnership agreement, have a solid assessment of the fiscal health of the practice, and use objective data to ensure that you pay fair market value for the practice.

Insights on private practice after 26 years and the dawn of the Internet.

J. Robert Wyatt, M.D.

I was flattered to be asked by Joe to add my thoughts to such an interesting and insightful book. As a Vanderbilt graduate, I was surprised to learn that 'Bama grads can read and write! Who knew! Must have been the Washington and Lee education...

But in all seriousness...

I am an Otolaryngologist, and as such view practice through the lens of someone who cares for both adults and children, and who's practice is about 25% surgical. My thoughts and advice on the business of medicine may therefore not be entirely appropriate for everyone in every practice setting. Keep in mind however that almost all of Joe's are.

Joe's advice on investing and building a tribe is excellent, and I can really add very little other than to say that you should read these chapters carefully and take the advice to heart. I would add that I recommend that you keep some amount of discretionary investment funds set aside for high risk / high reward investments related to your practice, such as surgery centers, owning the real estate of your office, and so on. Things are going to come up that are legitimate but high-risk investments related to your field and you should set yourself up so you can take advantage of them. As Joe has said elsewhere in this book, do your due diligence before investing, especially your legal due diligence. Many investments and deals that look perfectly fine from a simple common-sense standpoint can run afoul of regulations that could cause you big trouble. Prosecutors have argued, successfully, in court, that you were taught all the anti-kickback and other relevant laws in medical school and have no excuse for breaking even the most esoteric regulations.

I have another important philosophical point to add about business, investing, and physicians.

We have thorough our education, training and careers been taught never to quit. Good advice for a surgeon. Bad advice for an investor. A decision to stop throwing good money after bad, or to resign from an administrative position where you have no control but lots of responsibility is not quitting. It is cutting your losses. Don't let others take advantage of your commitment and dedication.

So on to the reason why Joe asked me to contribute to his book. Traditionally, practice success has been defined by "ability, affability, and availability". This has been true since the 1960's and long before.

Ability – an obvious criterion, you can get the job done with expected or better than expected results. Affability – you are pleasant to deal with, communicate well, and can be relied on. Availability – critical in the early stages of one's career, you are there when others need you. Meeting these three standards was enough in the past to ensure success, particularly for specialists, as most if not all the patients would come from referrals from other doctors.

Now referrals come from three sources, four as you become more established. Referrals from other doctors remain very important. As you become established patient "word of mouth" becomes important, and I would estimate 25-30% of my patients now come from former patients who are happy with what I have done to people they know. But two new categories of patient referrals have become very important and worthy of careful attention.

The first is "network" referrals. If you are an employed physician, it is likely the majority if not nearly all of your patients will come from this source at the start. Patients sent to you because you are part of some sort of "health network" controlled by a health system. Examples include the Northwell system in greater NYC, Sutter in Northern California, Memorial Healthcare in Houston. In theory, a "clinically integrated network of providers dedicated to cost-effective high quality care." Cynically, a legal referral scheme to force the PCP's to only refer to specialists who will utilize diagnostic and surgical facilities that are part of the system. This is important in that you must be aware of the rules and expectations of the system and the PCPs, as well as practicing top notch care. For example, doing a great job while utilizing the wrong imaging center, or failing to log in regularly to the proper EMR system, can cause you to be labeled a "low quality" physician. You do not want this. So, make sure you understand the expectations of everyone involved be sure to meet them. In this day and age, you must do more than just practice good medicine. Once upon a time, we had monthly conferences on medicine, surgery and anesthesia. Although these still do happen occasionally, we now spend most of our time on computer software training and procedures to ensure compliance with these issues.

If you are not employed, or if you are employed but have some control and discretion over your marketing budget and marketing program, internet referrals have become a major source of patient volume, particularly over the last 7-10 years. Many if not all patients who you see have already studied you on Google before they show up at your door, and many of those were initially referred to another physician and came to you because of more favorable reviews, or a superior internet presence otherwise, such as better photos, video, or other media. As surprising as this may be to some of you, my experience has recently been confirmed by a prominent health policy and quality measurement organization. A recent survey from Press Ganey, www.pressganey.com, reported that online reviews and star ratings are the most important factor in choosing a new healthcare provider. According to the data, this online information is more important to consumers than another doctor's referral and is more than twice as important when choosing a primary care physician. 83% of respondents said they went online to read reviews of a physician after being referred. In choosing a new primary care doctor, 52% of respondents start with the web, using search engines, primarily Google, 65% of the time. Other sites used included WebMD, hospital sites, Healthgrades, and Facebook.

This is a very rapidly evolving area so it is difficult to be specific about numbers and day to day tactical strategy. Suffice it to say you should be working with an online marketing firm that accomplishes several key tasks.

First, they optimize your basic online presence, specifically your website. It should be up to date with information that is accurate. It should be optimized so it is at or near the top of searches for terms that your treat or would like to treat, such as leg pain, back pain, nasal congestion, snoring, headache, fertility, or whatever is relevant to you. You want patients in your area, looking for solutions to the problems you can solve, to easily find you.

Second, they need to manage reviews. This involves more than anything encouraging the patients who are happy with you to complete a favorable review for you. We have a firm that sends a text to every patient after every visit asking them how their visit was. If the response is favorable, we ask them to provide a review and provide a link. If not, we provide them with contact information for our office manager and resolve the issue.

If you do not actively manage your reviews, the negative reviews will dominate your online profile. If this happens, people researching you will see a distorted perspective of your practice, as unhappy patients are tenfold (or more) more likely to write a review than happy patients.

Once we were able to accomplish the above, my practice settled into a pattern that has held for several years now where almost 30% of my practice is based on my favorable online appearance. I see dozens of patients every month who are referred to a specific specialist, but after conducting online "research" decide to come see me.

Dr. Robert Wyatt is a Board Certified Otolaryngologist (ENT specialist) in private practice in suburban Dallas, Texas. He received his M.D. and a M.B.A. at Vanderbilt University in Nashville and completed surgery and otolaryngology residency training at the Johns Hopkins Hospital in Baltimore Maryland. Outside of the direct practice of medicine, he has grown his solo practice into a practice with four doctors, plus a physician's assistant, and over the years has served as chief medical officer for a small hospital system, a board member and chair of the board for a local surgery center, and on a number of advisory and policy committees for various medical organizations.

Chapter III
Medical Billing Economics/ How Physicians Bill & Collect and Why this is Important

Billing and Coding Quick Tutorial

For those new to practice, the following is a step-by-step guide on how the revenue cycle process works in a medical practice. For those currently in practice, it is suggested that you don't skip over this section because it presents an excellent opportunity to ensure that your practice is following best practices.

Terminology To Know:

EMR: Electronic Medical Records- Clinical Documentation

PM: Practice Management- Billing System

CPT: Current Procedural Terminology / Procedure and Visit Codes (99212, 99203, J7321, 20610)

ICD-10: Diagnosis (M19.90)

Remittance: Another word for payment. It is defined as a sum of money sent, especially by mail, in payment for goods or services

Revenue Cycle Process (in short form):

1) Starts with a patient presenting his/her insurance card and staff entering the information into the system.

2) Insurance should be verified to ensure that it is active, obtain plan benefits, check to see if the provider is in/out of network and if a referral or authorization is needed.

3) The physician will see the patient and diagnose the patient. Then he/she will perform any testing as deemed necessary. Some procedures will require authorizations before performing the service.

4) The physician will need to place the CPT (visit code/procedure code) and diagnosis in the chart for the billers.

5) The billers will review the claim, scrub it, and batch it to go out. "Scrubbing" means to review the CPT/DX and add any modifiers needed and ensure that the correct codes are used on the claim before it goes out.

6) The payer receives the claims and sends them back to the practice. The billers retrieve the remittance and post the payment per the remittance, or they work the claim if it is denied. Additionally, they batch and send statements to patients who owe after the remittance is processed fully.

7) A patient billing account is closed out when all claims have been resolved.

Specific Revenue Process Steps

1) Doctor receives a faxed referral and/or patient calls for an appointment

2) Doctor scheduling staff schedules the appointment

3) Doctor staff must verify <u>eligibility</u>, <u>benefits,</u> and <u>referrals/ authorizations</u> prior to appointment.

This is the most important aspect and beginning of the RCM (Revenue Cycle Management) Process. Remember, you can see 100 patients a day, but if you don't verify (eligibility, benefits, and referral/prior authorizations <u>see below</u>) and collect properly, those 100 patients mean nothing to your collections!

Eligibility:

o Make sure the plan is **active** (Obtain Effective and Term Date of the Plan)

o Verify the information that the scheduler took is correct; **any** of these details can cause a claim to deny. Insurance Plan (Aetna PPO/HMO), Subscriber ID, Group number, Subscriber Name and DOB, Insured Name, and DOB.

o Make sure the plan entered above is **In-Network** with the specific provider/facility treating the patient.

You can check benefits all day long, but if you don't verify eligibility, the benefits are useless.

Benefits:

o Obtain Copay, Deductible, and Coinsurance information for expected services

o When obtaining benefits ensure that there are no plan exclusions for certain   services

Referral/ Authorization:

o Verify that the plan does not require a referral or authorization prior to being seen. *All HMOs will require a referral; some EPO (exclusive provider organization) plans require this. Every plan must be checked!*

o If the plan requires authorization, the office staff must call the PCP (primary care provider) to initiate the authorization and authorization must be obtained "prior" to being seen.

Note: **Referrals** *in 'insurance terminology' means a referral/authorization number, not simply a written/verbal referral from another physician. It **must be** a referral issued to you from the insurance company.*

Eligibility, benefits, and referrals/authorization are all performed prior to the patient being seen. These are the most important steps and if they are not done correctly, you are taking the chance of not getting paid by the insurance company and do not expect the patient to pay for the full service out of pocket. With new laws like the No Surprise Billing Act, you cannot just bill out of network without notifying the patient at least three days prior to the service.

4. The patient is seen by the doctor and the doctor and/or coder codes the procedures and visits performed. For example: New Visit: 99203, Cortisone Injection & Administration: J1100/20610 RT.

5. The billing company receives the physician's dictation and coding, and it is scrubbed by the biller. This means that the billers make sure that the correct codes are used, and they add any modifiers needed.

6. The billing company batches and sends the claim to the clearinghouse.

    o The clearinghouse is a software that payers use to process the claims. The clearinghouse will preliminarily scrub claims and kick them out. For example, it will kick out claims with incorrect Payer ID/Subscriber Info Mismatch. From this point, billers work those.

    o Other claims are passed through the clearinghouse and sent from the clearinghouse to the payer.

7. The payer receives the claim and processes it.

    o Claim is paid – Billers make any adjustments needed (payer fee schedule) and post payment, clearing the account to zero or billing the patient any cost-sharing portion (copay,

Chapter 3 - Medical Billing Economics/How Physicians Bill & Collect and Why this is Important

---

deductible, coinsurance) *Note: If your staff did a good job of verifying benefits, the patient should not owe.*

- o Claim is denied - Billers work it and resend the claim with corrections.

- o Claim requests more info - Billers work it and send additional information that the payer requests.

- o At month-end, billers batch patient statements and send those to the patients for any cost-sharing portions left on the AR. *Note: Every office can create its own AR process specific to its requests and needs.*

8. Claim is processed by the payer, worked by the billing team, and patient is billed for any outstanding AR or patient payments are applied to the account to clear the account to ZERO.

9. The end of the revenue cycle is when each claim is cleared to zero.

Coding:

Step 4 in the revenue cycle process is coding and it warrants further discussion. First, coding is when a provider or coder determines what level a visit is, or what services were performed and chooses the appropriate CPT code for those services. Additionally, providers must understand what diagnosis will cover certain procedures. Example: If a physician wants to bill a viscosupplementation injection, there are only certain diagnoses that will cover that injection. If a provider doesn't bill the appropriate diagnosis and doesn't check to see if the injection requires prior authorization, then the claim could be denied so it is important to learn the functions of billing to increase revenues.

There are two ways of coding that are traditionally employed:

1) Physician coding his/her own work. Physicians really have become their own coders, and this is something that they are often not told or taught during medical school.

2) A physician can hire a coder, but then it starts with the physician dictating/documenting properly for the coder to catch what is performed.

Note: It is a fact that physicians can code more precisely than a hired coder since they are the ones rendering the services, whereas coders must rely on the documentation of a provider; and providers are not known for documenting thoroughly.

Example:
CPT: Visit and Procedural Codes (99212, 99203, J7321, 20610)
ICD-10: Diagnosis (M19.90)
Put CPT and DX codes together (99212, M19.90)

Documentation:
Make sure your documentation meets standards for billing (new billing guidelines are always being updated).

Coding Compliance

It is highly recommended that you employ a third party to perform a coding compliance audit every year. This recommendation holds regardless of whether you are employed or in private practice. These audits will typically review twenty to twenty-five random claims selected and provide feedback to you and your business team so you may respond. Note that coding is inherently subjective, and the results should be discussed as a way for you and your staff to improve and achieve best practices; however, this does not negate the need for the audit.

Chapter 3 - Medical Billing Economics/How Physicians Bill & Collect and Why this is Important

Improper coding has ramifications, and they are all adverse:

1. If you are under coding, you are leaving money on the table and not compliantly maximizing your revenue, and hence income.

2. If you are upcoding, it carries severe penalties. All insurance companies have screens that profile cases and physicians. If you are using a high reimbursing code that is reserved for specific outlier patients, and this is the regular code you are using, the claim will likely either be denied, and/or the plan medical director will call you, or you will be dropped from that managed care plan. It is not atypical for a physician to be dropped from a plan. Depending on the payer, this could have a severe impact on your practice.

3. If you are upcoding, regardless of whether you are aware of it, you could be subject to *criminal* penalties. Under the federal False Claims Act, upcoding crimes lead to **incarceration of up to five years and fines worth up to $250,000**. There are also state laws that typically follow the federal laws that are additional to the federal penalties if convicted.

As a close to the coding topic, as mentioned previously, improper coding is a common way that physicians find themselves being prosecuted. Another is the federal anti-kickback act that prohibits receiving remuneration (money paid for work or service) for the referral of any service potentially reimbursable under a federal healthcare program. See Appendix III. Two non-physicians in Texas contrived a scheme to pay physicians to order multi-level drug screens on patients having surgery. Typically, an eight-level drug screen is run on patients where the physician suspects drug usage that could cause complications during surgery. This happens occasionally. A 100+ level screen that is typically only used for vehicular homicides is rarely ordered for surgical patients. The promoters who owned the lab contrived a scheme where the referring physicians would be paid a percentage of the lab revenue from the drug screen for non-federal or state-funded patients. The physicians were encouraged to order the 100+ level drug screen for all patients since it reimburses much higher than the eight-level screen to maximize their income. Note that ordering any of these screens is an anomaly and, in this instance, 80-year-old patients who were receiving cataract surgery (non-intubated surgery with nearly zero risk of aspiration) were receiving 100+ level drug screens. This resulted in a $300 million lawsuit by United Healthcare (now Optum) against the promoters and potential federal criminal penalties and state penalties for those involved. As a coda, the promoters were convicted of federal crimes and are now serving sentences for yet another scheme. The physicians may be subject to penalties and exclusion from the UHC plans. The lesson from this is the physicians were knowingly ordering tests that they were told were "compliant" by the promoters even though they knew they were unnecessary and the physicians' received kickbacks through this arrangement. Two laws were broken that could have easily been identified by your attorney, business advisor, and coding audit company.

Compliance (including the federal anti-kickback statute and other topics) is further discussed in Appendix III but use your judgment and common sense.

> CONCEPT 5: Coding compliance is a serious topic and one of the most common ways that physicians get into trouble. Use a third-party coding company as a protection against this and follow their recommendations unless you strongly disagree with them. In that instance, obtain another coding audit to act as the decider. Making a concerted effort to be compliant is essential.

Chapter IV
Understanding Financial Statements

Throughout your career, you will be presented with financial statements. From experience, most physicians have a general understanding of them but do not have an in-depth knowledge of how to interpret them. Financial statements are only as good as the data received so the "garbage in, garbage out" analogy applies. For this discussion, we will assume that the financials are presented accurately but will touch on how to spot red flags and steps to take to protect you from that type of malfeasance.

First and foremost, please do not be intimidated or worse, ambivalent to them. Using a medical correlation, they are the most effective tool to assess the fiscal health of your practice because they allow you to do a diagnostic of your practice and identify specific areas that require attention. Once you pinpoint an issue, there are usually only a few reasons for the anomaly, allowing you and your team to go about systematically and methodically "treating" the issue.

Chapter 4 - Understanding Financial Statements

Example: You are in a group practice and discover that your collections per patient are lower than your partners who practice in another location.[1] With this issue identified you and your business manager can take the necessary steps to address the problem. In this instance, it could be a different payer mix (percentage of Medicaid/Medicaid to commercial insurance patients) due to practicing in a different location. If that is not the issue, you should check your insurance contracts and make sure that Blue Cross, for example, is reimbursing you at the same rate as your partners and if they are not, you should contact your Blue Cross representative and managed care consultant to address reimbursement. If neither of these is identified as problems, you may have an issue in your business office with your revenue cycle systems so you must confirm that: claims are going out cleanly (See Coding above), eligibility, benefits, and referrals/authorizations systems prior to the appointment are in place, insurance denials are being worked, and co-pays and deductibles are being collected. In summary, the point of this example is that you use the financials to pinpoint issues in your practice and without an understanding of how to use financial statements, the physician in this example could be losing a tremendous amount of money that compounds over time because he or she did not take the time to understand how to interpret financials to improve their practice. You cannot just rely on your business manager to do this; you must do it too.

We recommend that you have your accountant publish monthly financials. If you are employed in a large group practice this may not be applicable because the practice or health system will publish them. However, note that it is a check and balance on your practice administrator and allows for a third party to prepare the financials and ask questions. Once they are published, a monthly review of the financials should be conducted with the practice administrator and/or business advisor. This should include benchmark data for the

---

[1] This type of data (collections per patient) is comparative data and is essential to assist you run your practice. In fact, benchmarks are a major point of emphasis so you can compare yourself with similar physicians and practices. That data is readily available through the Medical Group Management Association.

month and for longer periods to show trending. Just be aware that there are monthly fluctuations due to the seasonality of healthcare so quarterly and yearly data is typically most helpful to show key trends.

> CONCEPT 6: What gets measured, gets done. A monthly, quarterly, and yearly review of benchmarks and financial statements to identify areas of improvement or anomalies is a fundamental and essential strategy for running your practice and alerts your internal team that practice efficiency is a priority.

Financial Statement Reporting

It should be noted that there are two ways of reporting financial statements. The cash method and the accrual method. The cash method recognizes revenue/collections and expenses when they are received and paid respectively. The accrual method attempts to match up revenue/collections and expenses with the month incurred. For example, you see a record number of patients in December and are paid in early February. Under the *cash method*, the revenue is recognized on your February financials, or when it is received. Under the *accrual method*, the revenue from that patient is recognized in December using the expected reimbursement rates from your managed care contracts or Medicare/Medicaid. The weakness of cash accounting is that under the above scenario, for example, it appears that the physician had a busy February when in reality, December was extremely busy. The second weakness is due to the delay in payment, you and your manager will not recognize issues on your financials until 30 to 45 days later whereas any anomalies become apparent under the accrual method due to matching revenues and expenses for the month incurred.

Notwithstanding, most physician practices are on the *cash method* of accounting, and this works if the *accounts receivable* (money owed to you by insurance companies and patients) are tracked very carefully. Accounts receivable management is performed by taking the accounts receivable and dividing them into "buckets" based on the age of the claim. For example, any claim outstanding that is 30 days or less is considered current but claims over 30 days require attention, and the business staff should perform calls and follow up with the patients or insurance companies to collect monies owed. Regular review of your accounts receivable (claims outstanding) is critical and there should be no write-offs on accounts unless you and your practice manager acquiesce.

What you should look for in a Bank

By Christina Fanning, Vice President ServisFirst Bank

Your primary goal when looking for a bank is to find one focused on commercial banking with a full suite of cash management solutions emphasizing competitive products, a strong technology platform, and that is dedicated to quality service.

Banks are many times thought of in two ways. The first is a community type bank with great customer service, but it somehow lacks the assets needed to provide a strong technology platform. The second type is a large, retail bank with a strong product suite and technology, but it is sorely lacking in personalized customer service. Today, however, there are full-service commercial banks with enough assets that they can invest in technology and have strength in size, without being so large that everything is governed by bureaucracy, which makes it difficult to get things done. These banks are able to offer the best of both worlds.

You will need a bank that understands business; this is especially true in the medical field where there may not be many tangible assets against which to borrow. Banks that focus on large numbers of clients tend to get bogged down by volume, and clients are serviced by a 1-800 number or are left waiting in line for answers. During the recent Paycheck Protection Program (PPP), banks which were successful in obtaining loans for their clients were only able to do so because they were large enough to implement good technology, yet small enough not to get buried underneath needless bureaucratic red tape. If you look at the banks that performed well for their clients and provided the largest number of loans it was the ones that had relationships with their clients, and were dedicated to helping them.

The importance of technology should not be underestimated. A good online banking platform saves time and headache. With the right technology you never have to physically go to the bank; everything you need can be accessed through your computer or phone. A bank should also offer products that provide fraud protection, which is rampant in today's environment.

What you should look for in a Banker

It is vital that you have a dedicated relationship manager/banker/lender at your bank; someone who will give you their cell phone and answer when you call. You need a banker that is cognizant of your busy schedule and will come to you if needed. You need a banker that understands business and has experience working with others in the medical field. Your banker should offer competitive terms with rates and fees that are priced fairly.

These preferred bankers work for banks that give them the tools to effectively serve their clients. They have strong, experienced teams that support them and allow them to respond quickly to your needs. They can expedite requests and get things done for their clients.

They will offer you a term sheet for new lending transactions and spend time reviewing what the terms mean to you. They will offer ongoing guidance and will be a resource to you as you make business decisions. Your banker should be someone who works well with the other members of your team; accountants and bankers communicate frequently.

It is important to remember banking is about a relationship and not a specific transaction. While terms are important, you also need to think about who will be working with you day in and day out.

Christina Fanning is a Vice President, Private Banking Officer, with ServisFirst Bank in Birmingham, Alabama. She works with commercial clients providing relationship management and lending expertise. She graduated Cum Laude from the University of Alabama with a Bachelor of Science in Commerce and Business Administration and also completed professional studies at New York University. Fanning is active in her community, serving on the board of her rotary club in addition to several other non-profit boards. She can be reached at CFanning@servisfirstbank.com

CONCEPT 7: Your collections are your fiscal lifeline so ensuring that sound processes are in place and those processes are working is essential. Maintaining those systems using your accountant, practice manager, and business advisor is a crucial part of being a successful practicing physician.

Using Benchmarks Effectively

Benchmark data is mentioned frequently in this book and for good reason. One of the best ways to spot malfeasance, graft, or mismanagement is to observe a practice not adhering to reasonable benchmarks. As stated above, key practice benchmark data is readily available and thus, regular financial benchmark review must be part of your practice plan. While you can do it monthly, quarterly and yearly data presents the most accurate picture. This data is a key check and balance, and these reviews should involve your practice manager, accountant, and business advisor.

Sample benchmarks

- Number of patient encounters per provider

- Revenue per patient per provider

- Total Overhead as a % of Revenue – these are your practice's expenses divided by your collections.

- Days in Accounts Receivable – how many days it takes to collect your accounts receivable (what patients and insurers owe you).

- Bad Debt – these are write-offs of accounts. It is important to measure this because excessive write-offs are a source of graft (the employee writes off the account but pockets the money) or an indication that accounts are not being worked and collected properly.

- Total Accounts Receivable and Revenue by Provider – comparative data with your partners and the benchmarks

- Rejection and Denial Rate – see write-offs but this also measures that the verification process is working.

- Average hold time, average wait time, average time to appointment for new and established patients.

Practice Audits/Revenue Cycle Management (revisited)

A final note, and important note, about revenue cycle management. Revenue is like oxygen for your practice so you must ensure that it is being maximized in a compliant manner. The only way to do this is by independently verifying. It is recommended that you utilize an independent third party to conduct three audits:

1. Coding Audit
2. Billing/Collecting Audit
3. Internal Control Review

To be specific, for those employed by a health system, the billing, coding, and collecting (revenue cycle functions) are typically performed offsite at a central location operated by the health system whereas private practices either perform the revenue cycle functions internally or use a third-party billing company.

For private practice, either approach (in-house revenue cycle or outsourced) works as long as there are checks and balances in place. Specifically, if the revenue cycle functions are performed in-house, regular coding audits must be performed annually for compliance (See Coding above). Secondly, billing and collecting audits are performed so you verify that the key revenue cycle functions are being performed properly. Similar to coding audits, twenty or thirty claims are pulled randomly and tracked by the auditor. This is not costly and provides a positive indication of the performance of your revenue cycle systems. Third, an operational/internal control audit is performed to check internal controls to protect against graft and ensure that operating systems are working. The internal control audit should be conducted every three years or sooner if the benchmark data suggests problems. If using a billing company, the same recommendations apply so make sure you have annual coding and billing audits. Your business advisor or practice manager will identify firms that will perform these audits. Finally, for those employed, you must insist on third-party verification that the revenue cycle functions are operating properly. Note that medical practice benchmark data is the best indicator of this so independently verify (or ask your business advisor) by running a simple benchmark check on key management factors.

Chapter V
Creating and Interacting with your Tribe: Part II

In Chapter 1, the discussion centered on building your *Internal Tribe* or the people you interact with daily and how working effectively with them as a team or pack perpetuates everyone's interest. Remember the wolfpack hunting analogy whereby the pack hunts as a group because working in cohesion achieves the most success? That Internal Tribe is how you are most effective in building your practice. In the next two chapters, we discussed interacting with people, choosing your practice using strategic considerations, negotiating your compensation, negotiating your employment agreement and/or partnership agreement, and the revenue cycle process. To analogize this to sports, the first part of this book was centered on how to score – building your practice, learning to be effective and efficient, not committing penalties (compliance), and working with your teammates (Internal Tribe) to be successful. However, defense is critical to winning championships and this chapter's focus is on how to protect your interests and maintain a solid practice.

As a physician, you are asked to effectively negotiate your compensation, evaluate a practice to join, assess real estate opportunities, decide whether to invest in a surgery center or similar healthcare

Chapter 5 - Creating and Interacting with your Tribe: Part II

venture, determine if your practice is efficient and maximizing its revenue potential, determine if your practice is controlling expenses based on similar practices, evaluate your managers and staff and ensure they are not stealing from you, evaluate loans, evaluate contractual arrangements, purchase the correct type and amount of insurance and…….my experience if that very few know how to do this and practice medicine. The solution is to extend your Tribe - build a team or walls around you to protect you and your interests. We call this developing and perpetuating your *External Tribe*.

Managing Legal Counsel
By: Charles A. Omage, Esq.

As an attorney who now operates a private real estate company and manages attorneys on a daily basis, I was honored and pleased that Joe asked me to contribute to this book. We all know that hiring good attorneys is important, and there are a myriad of choices of law firms, but few truly understand how to identify the most optimal attorney to handle their specific needs. Additionally, and as importantly, your attorneys must be managed properly, just as any of your other advisors or team members, in order to achieve your objectives in an efficient and cost-effective manner. With this in mind, the following are just a few tips and suggestions based on my experience.

1. **Select a "Business Lawyer":** There are hundreds if not thousands of firms who have expertise in health care law. However, not all lawyers think like "business lawyers". By that, I mean someone who not only has significant subject matter expertise, but who also clearly understands your business objectives and does not over-negotiate or get bogged down in legal details that may not matter. In addition, I would recommend that you select an attorney or law firm that consists of a "one stop shop" for healthcare legal needs. Not only will you need a general healthcare attorney, but you will also need expertise in related areas, such as corporate, privileges, tax, anti-kickback, fraud and malpractice. It is my experience that, while there certainly are exceptions, having separate attorneys in multiple firms working for you is more time consuming to manage, inefficient and expensive. I would advise that you seek recommendations from your colleagues and advisors, as well from local physician organizations.

2. **Set Expectations:** While selecting the most expensive attorney or law firm may assure you competent representation, it does not necessarily translate to a prudent decision. For example, would you select a $1,000 per hour Wall Street firm to handle your house closing, or would it make more sense to select a competent residential real estate attorney who charges a fixed price of $500? Think about your specific needs and goals, as well as your financial standing, before you select an attorney.

In addition, don't be afraid to have very direct conversations about your expectations, including not only legal goals, but also the price you're willing to pay for the achievement of such goals. Ask your attorney to prepare a budget up front, and if possible, in such a form that allows you to approve tasks on an individual basis, so that you can effectively managing your costs, while achieving your legal objectives.

3. **Consider Alternative Fee Structures:** Typically, attorneys and law firm bill on an hourly basis. While this structure is certainly sensible, it may not be the optimal structure for your situation. As part of your selection process, I would ask the attorney or law firm to present you with alternative fee structures, such as fixed fees, fee caps, contingent fees or hybrids of different structures. For example, some attorneys will handle employment contracts on a fixed fee basis, and others will handle litigation on a contingent fee basis. Think about your legal needs and financial capabilities and request to see a menu of billing options tailored to the same.

4. **Engage in Oversight:** Regardless of the attorney or law firm you select, and notwithstanding their billing structure, you will almost always have to manage them closely to keep your legal expenses in check. However, here are a few tips that will provide guardrails on your attorneys on the front end, to keep their billing in control:

    a. **Clarify staffing in your engagement letter (more on this below).** Staffing should be clear and limited on the front end of the engagement, meaning who is working on your file and their respective billing rates. Ideally, the lower-priced attorney (associate) or paralegal (in some cases) should be handling the simpler tasks while the more senior attorney (partner) should be in more of an oversight role while handling the more complex tasks. Unless the matter is extremely large and complex, across multiple legal disciplines, it should never be staffed by more than one partner, one associate and one paralegal.

    b. **Utilize task management.** If possible, separate your engagement into separate and distinct tasks, with a budget for each. This will provide more transparency as to deadline expectations and the costs associated with each task. It also allows you to easily stop the attorneys from moving forward with a subsequent task if you are not satisfied with the work or cost associated with a prior task.

c. **Require Periodic Reporting.** Regardless of the billing structure you agree to, you should require detailed periodic reports at a minimum, which describe the fees/costs as well as the tasks performed with respect to the same. This will allow you to red flag any items that may seem excessive or out of budget earlier in the process. Nobody wants the stress of sticker shock at the conclusion of the representation, and so periodic and transparent reporting is key to managing expenses throughout the engagement. I would request monthly reporting at a minimum.

In conclusion, identifying the right attorney or law firm for your specific needs is critical, and it is not always the "best" or "smartest" or "most expensive" attorney that is optimal for your needs. Take the time to assess your objectives and financial capabilities, and select a firm that brings the two together. Carefully vet the attorneys or law firms that you find or who are recommended to you, and require that many of the items I set forth above (expectations, staffing, billing structures, reporting, etc.) be specifically set forth in your formal engagement letter with the attorney or law firm. Joe makes an exemplary point in saying "What gets measured, gets done," and I want to emphasize this because, in my opinion, you will obtain the best results by managing your counsel closely, having full transparency and developing an honest and collaborative relationship.

Charles A. Omage is Executive Vice President and Principal Member of Barber Partners, LLC, a Dallas-based real estate investment and operating company. Charles is responsible for overseeing all transactional, capital markets and legal activities of the company, including the structuring and negotiation of project investments and debt and equity capital transactions, as well as risk management and general legal oversight. He can be reached at charles.omage@icloud.com

Building Your External Tribe

Playing good defense is about collecting people with very specific skill sets and aligning with them. Picture yourself as the king of your kingdom. How do you keep your kingdoms safe and remain on the throne? The answer is clear - build high walls around your castle and a deep moat to protect your interests from those who want what you have (hint: your wealth). *The solution is to build a team of trusted advisors and create a system of checks and balances to protect you and accomplish your financial and personal goals.* The concept of division of labor applies whereby different people have diverse talents. Remember, you don't know everything, and there is no shame not knowing about taxes or depreciation or negotiating contracts. Very few can transition between the two worlds of business and practicing medicine.

Your Internal Tribe: The Essential Team of Core Advisors and their Roles

- **Business Advisor** – your business advisor should act as the ringmaster to identify and coordinate your advisors, make sure your practice is benchmarked and audited, and you are staying the course with your investment plan. For example, your business advisor should help you build your Internal Tribe by vetting advisors for you. He or she should also maintain a practice plan for you that ensures that there are internal control audits performed to ensure that there is no graft, the essential coding audits are performed (See Coding Compliance above), billing audits are performed, your practice financials are reviewed and benchmarked, and your investment plan is being followed. Finally, if you use an investment or wealth manager, the business advisor should ensure that the investment manager is truly adding value, acting as a fiduciary, not churning the account (making excessive trades), and maintaining the risk profile that you selected. It is very important that your business advisor only be compensated by you and act as a fiduciary to you. A *fiduciary* has an obligation

Chapter 5 - Creating and Interacting with your Tribe: Part II

to look out for your interests and put your interests ahead of theirs. This is the same as a trustee who oversees a trust and has a fiduciary obligation to the trust. Put another way, your business advisor should only be compensated by you and not receive referral fees from advisors he or she suggests you use.[2] As stated above, the business advisor acts as your coordinator over your tribe and typically charges an hourly fee for services or a monthly fee. The check on your business advisor is your accountant who will objectively evaluate the performance of your practice. If your practice is failing or underperforming, your business advisor should be proactive in advising you.

- **Attorney** – Attorneys have different core competencies within the law and specialize in areas such as trial, commercial and corporate, human resources, estate planning, healthcare, tax, and family law. They are a key part of your internal tribe. You will require expertise in many of these areas such as assistance with structuring your practice, negotiating the legal aspects of your employment agreement, negotiating the legal aspects of your partnership agreement, and reviewing and advising on human resource issues amongst other things. In addition to a general business attorney, a healthcare regulatory expert may be helpful if you, or any entity you are involved with, are entering into an arrangement that will provide ancillary income such as an ambulatory surgery center investment or similar arrangement. See <u>Appendix III</u> and the compliance discussion above. You want your own attorney to consult and issue an opinion, if for nothing else to clearly document that you consulted an attorney to make sure you were following the regulations. As your practice matures and your income and wealth increase, you may require estate planning and tax law assistance. The law is constantly changing, and employment law is an area where you will also require expertise. Insurance for employment practices and malpractice claims is

---

[2] As full disclosure, ASD Management provides business advisory services, and this evolved out of student requests.

discussed below but be aware that if you are sued, the insurance company will appoint an attorney to handle the claim. Regardless, this does not negate the need for legal expertise that represents your interest and not the insurance company. Furthermore, sound legal advice acts as a prophylactic to help deter lawsuits.

Legal advice is expensive and can vary from $250 to $800 per hour on average. The check on your attorney is your accountant and business advisor who will monitor billing practices and contrast that with their other clients. You want attorneys who play the "long game" and see you as a long-term client and thus, do not "scorch the earth" with their billing. It is key that your attorney is aware your accountant or business advisor is reviewing the legal bills.

How do you choose an attorney? It is recommended that you identify a firm with a strong healthcare practice that also has other areas of expertise so you have partners within that firm that can consult with you on non-healthcare-related issues discussed above. A local or regional firm may be a good option as you build your referral network and interact with potential patients. Your business advisor is a good resource to identify firms because he or she will likely have experience working with different laws firms and can evaluate the best fit for you.

- **Accountant** – we advise hiring a CPA (Certified Public Accountant) that has numerous physician clients and specializes in healthcare. The CPA has many roles: the primary role is to prepare tax returns and advise on tax matters such as withholding for taxes and deductions. The accountant may also advise on purchases and practice matters. A key role is auditing or performing internal reviews of your practice and your practice administrator. Another key role is to perform checks on your financial/estate planner, business advisor, and attorney. The check on the accountant is your lawyer to ensure no duplicity with other advisors and ensure your accountant is taking a measured but non-aggressive approach to tax planning. Your business advisor who if not your attorney is another check on your CPA.

How do you choose an accountant? As stated above, use an accountant with a healthcare practice. Your business advisor can help identify one or you can network through your colleagues to identify. We recommend using a medium to a large accounting firm that provides expertise in different areas of accounting. Because accounting is similar to the law in that different areas require different expertise such as tax, estate planning, audit, and business consulting, our experience is that it is extremely helpful for your accountant to be able to consult with his or her partners on different areas and this is why we recommend larger specialized healthcare accounting firms.

- **Ancillary Business Manager** – they will manage nontraditional investments such as surgery centers, or real estate partnerships. Your attorney and accountant are the best checks on them. It is essential that financial information be disclosed and sent to your accountant and attorney so they can compare and contrast with similar ventures. Insist on the right to audit. The ancillary businesses are very important supplemental income sources, and the key is working with trusted and competent managers who have a long and successful track record. When evaluating ancillary ventures, you must do third-party verification regarding their background and claimed results such as calling references and having your attorney do lien and litigation searches. We discuss this in detail under Ancillary Investments.

- **Marketing Consultant** – an important player on your team is a marketing consultant who will develop a website, manage SEO (Search Engine Optimization) and paid searches, and do a variety of things to manage online reputation, in particular Google reviews. Your website is your front door now and the reviews drive referrals. An estimated 1/3 of your patients are likely to come from your web presence. Choosing a marketing consultant is easier than some of the other advisors because they can show you other websites that they have designed. Ask for analytics and have them show you success rates. Your business advisor or practice manager should verify the analytics and verify references.

- **Insurance Agent** - a good *commercial insurance agent* will not only set you up with the proper coverages (malpractice, general liability, hired and non-owned, employment liability, cybersecurity, business interruption, directors and officers) but will meet with you regularly to assess your business and needs. They will be invaluable when you have a claim. Hire independent agents affiliated with firms who shop several carriers and are not tied to one carrier to achieve proper pricing. Hire agents who have healthcare experience. A common problem is being underinsured because your practice changes or there is a change in malpractice laws in your state and your agent is not engaged with you. You will also require a *personal insurance agent* to assist you with life insurance, disability insurance, homeowner and automobile policies. Again, it is recommended that you hire independent agents affiliated with firms who shop several carriers and are not tied to one carrier to achieve proper pricing. Insurance is discussed with specific recommendations later but please be aware that physicians are regularly approached by insurance agents. Insurance coverages that are required versus optional coverages can be confusing. As discussed above, understand motivations. Insurance agents are paid a percentage of the premium you pay so their incentive is to sell. This is not saying that agents are bad or practicing nefarious practices; rather, you must have a check and balance on their suggested coverages so you can purchase the policies that are best suited for you. Your business advisor and accountant are the best checks on them and finding a good broker who works in conjunction with the other members of your tribe is essential. How do you find a broker? Specializing in healthcare is essential. Similar to attorneys, identifying a firm that is independent and has resources that extend

Chapter 5 - Creating and Interacting with your Tribe: Part II

into other areas including analytics is very important. In sum, specialized insurance agents are a critical and valuable part of your tribe.

- **Banker** – an old joke: bankers love to loan you money when you don't need it and won't loan you money when you need it. Banks are not the same. The way to evaluate a bank is to determine your needs from that bank. For example, twenty years ago, having ATM locations and branches that were convenient was a major factor in choosing a bank. With online banking, this has waned. In the personal finance section, debt is discussed with the emphasis on limiting debt to only items that are essential (auto loans), items that historically appreciate (home loans), or generate income (school loans and business loans). A banker with whom you develop a close relationship is very important. For example, when COVID-19 impacted business in 2019-2020, the federal government issued payroll loans (PPP) through participating banks that were typically forgiven or carry low-interest rates if the borrower used the funds to keep staff employed. The large national bank that I worked with did not offer these loans. Fortunately, a friend of mine is the President of a regional bank and wrote the loan for me even though they were doing PPP loans only for "clients." I am a client now and moved my business to that bank. It really highlighted the need to have a personal banking relationship. Your banker is an integral part of your team because they know you and can respond in an emergency such as during the COVID-19 crisis or in the event of a natural disaster. The best check to make sure you are not overleveraged, or the interest rates offered are competitive is your CPA. See <u>What You Should Look For In A Banker</u>

- **Wealth Manager/Financial Advisor** – it is suggested that the role of a financial advisor is to help you meet your financial goals, assist with estate planning, assist you in assessing ancillary investments such as how real estate or how an investment in a healthcare business fits in your entire portfolio, and make sure you exercise financial constraint and don't make rash decisions. The misconception is that you turn your money over to the financial advisor and he or she picks stocks or funds. You can certainly do this, but we do not recommend it. In the Investment chapter below, we emphasize that beating the market on a long-term basis is nearly impossible and individual or institutional firms have yet to prove that they can beat the market without taking on disproportional risk, particularly after the cost of their fees, and the cost of trading and taxes generated by trading. The data proving this point is compelling and convincing. In fact, there is a whole industry centered on the fallacy that investors can "beat the market" with one of the more colorful outlets being CNBC. CNBC is financial pornography. Its job is to get you to watch and entertain. It will not help you beat the market because information regarding stocks and bonds is nearly instantaneously digested, and the market corrects and adjusts accordingly. Nearly every investment advisor claims that they can beat the market but few do in the long run (defined as your investment horizon of 35 to 40 years) and identifying that firm is impossible. The following are the questions to ask financial advisors:

o First, if your data suggests that you can beat the 'market,' how do you define the market? It should be a defined benchmark such as the Wilshire 5000 or the S&P 500 not an esoteric benchmark.

o The second question to ask is what time period is being measured? Ten years is fairly short, and the fact that nearly 70% of all mutual funds cannot beat the S&P 500 over a 20-year period is telling.

o The next question is if the returns generated actually beat the market and hence you can show you add value, how much risk is the physician investor taking in order to obtain these returns? Risk and return are linked, there is no free lunch. Over time higher returns can be generated but it nearly always requires additional risk and whether or not the physician is comfortable with that risk is a key

Chapter 5 - Creating and Interacting with your Tribe: Part II

---

question. In the <u>Investment</u> chapter, we provide a chart of historical returns using different risk levels.

o   The next question is how is the advisor compensated? Is it based on trades or the value of the portfolio? If on trades, the incentive is to trade securities. If on the value of the portfolio, the fee charged can vary from 0.25% to 1.50%. Please distinguish a wealth managers fee with the fee paid to a mutual fund manager. They are different but cumulative is you use a money manager. A money manager oversees your portfolio and picks stocks, bonds and mutual funds or ETFs to meeting your goals. As you will see below, it is very hard to overcome fees and just as hard to pick funds that will outperform the market. In fact, the reason that nearly all mutual fund managers cannot beat the market (let's use the S&P 500) is that over time there is *regression to the mean*, or fund returns tend to clump together. Thus, a simple index fund that is passively managed (no mutual fund manager) that charges 0.08% has a huge advantage over a fund and managers who effectively charge 1.20%. If mutual fund managers cannot beat the market, why would you hire an investment firm to manage your portfolio if they cannot pick fund managers who will outperform? You end up paying the money manager a fee of 1.0% on average to manage your portfolio, and mutual fund managers another estimated 1.2% of your portfolio. This is significant in the long run. Example: if you start with $10,000 and contribute $83 per month at 9%, you will have $300,397 in 30 years; however, if you do the same but return only 7% because you paid a money manager and used actively managed mutual funds, you will end up with only $183,013. You will lose nearly 40% of the returns you will achieve by using a simple passively managed portfolio (See below <u>Portfolio Construction</u>).

o   Another question to ask centers on certifications. Are they licensed with FINRA (Formerly National Association of Securities Dealers) or registered with the Securities and Exchange Commission?

- o Does the advisor act as a fiduciary to his or her clients? If not, you understand their incentive and do not hire them. Only hire an advisor who is a *fiduciary* meaning the advisor is bound legally and ethically to act in your best interests, putting their clients' interests ahead of their own, with a duty to preserve good faith and trust. If they are a fiduciary, they must register with the SEC (Securities and Exchange Commission) and your business advisor should confirm it.

- o Does the firm just manage money, or does it sell investment products?

- o Does the firm provide ancillary planning services and/or family office services?

- o The final question, and the key question to ask, is whether the historical returns shown are after (net of) fees? Typically, they are not and there is a reason for this.

Many physicians feel they do not have the time or requisite expertise to manage their money. It is suggested in the Investment chapter below that a very reasonable solution is to make regular monthly contributions to low-cost indexed mutual funds. These are perfectly suited for most investors and this approach has historically provided above average returns over the long run while providing diversity and adjusting for risk over time. This is the advice that I give to my children and suggest you follow.

Please do not misinterpret this as diminishing the role of financial advisors. They are a critical part of your tribe. They can assist with advising on insurance, and estate matters. They can also help you stay the course and not make rash decisions such as selling your stock portfolio when the market adjusts downward or stopping your monthly investment plan when the market is going down. The best ones are a source of calm and reason and can assist you with your entire financial picture, not just your investment portfolio. Put another way, your financial advisor/wealth manager helps you *stay the course* and assists you with your entire financial plan. The check on them is for your business advisor or accountant to benchmark their fees and ensure they are adding value.

How do you find the right financial advisor? Again, only hire a fiduciary advisor - a legal standard that provides some protection since they are obligated to act in your best interests. However, that is a wide standard so use your business advisor, lawyer, and accountant to assist in identifying ones with a good track record. We also recommend strongly that you pay them an hourly fee and not a percentage of your portfolio for their services just like you pay your accountant, business advisor, and lawyers.

- **Credentialing and Managed Care Consultants** – these are commonly overlooked but a critical part of your team particularly if you are in private practice. Credentialing assistance ensures you are participating and importantly maintain participation with the managed care plans that are your revenue source. Payer or managed care contracting is your revenue lifeline and a professional negotiator that can assist you with rates can greatly augment your income. Another overlooked area where they will assist is a review of the contract language in the managed care plan contracts because payers can insert adverse language in contracts that limit your reimbursement or be unfavorable. Negotiating this language and what you are paid is very important; thus, payer contracting is your revenue lifeline so finding this expertise is extremely important. Frankly, good ones are hard to find since this is a very specific niche. Network with your colleagues or associations and use your tribe members to identify them. Your practice administrator will work with them and use financial benchmark information to ensure they are adding value.

Evaluating your Tribe

It is very important to evaluate your team at least annually. Time is a precious commodity particularly with a busy practice and it is easy to let this slip since there are probably several things you would rather do. However, it may be helpful to put this recommendation into a different and more familiar context. Insurance companies pay for screening colonoscopies as a protective measure against colon cancer because if a patient is screened regularly and the polyps are identified early, it greatly reduces the chances that the patient will have colon cancer or develop more serious conditions. Put another way, if you never change the oil on your car, do not be surprised if you have serious and very expensive auto repairs.

How do you evaluate your Tribe? It is suggested that you divide between business and personal.

- For business, meet with your practice manager and practice partners and go through accomplishments for the year, evaluate the growth of the practice, identify areas for growth next year, discuss how to better network with referring physicians, and discuss challenges that were confronted for the year. Have your practice manager explain the financials with special emphasis on how they benchmark with similar practices. Finally, evaluate the goals for the current year and whether nor not they were achieved.

- Separately, meet with your accountant and business advisor to validate the practice financials and benchmarks that your practice manager presented. This is an effective check and balance and a good time to prepare the evaluation of your practice manager looking at objective accomplishments. It is important to use objective data and have third-party input to equitably evaluate.

- With your practice manager and business advisor, set expectations for the following year for the practice and your practice manager as the implementor as well as your business advisor and coordinator. For example, is the practice plan being followed? Are the checks and balances in place? Are the third-party audits occurring regularly?

- With your practice manager and business advisor evaluate your staff.

On a personal level, you should also perform evaluations. Meet with your business advisor to discuss and evaluate members of your Tribe. Your business advisor should do this for you and report on the following:

- Attorneys – have they been timely responding to you with requests? Are their bills reasonable? Are they providing the services needed? Are they keeping you abreast of changes in the law that impact you or your practice?

- Banker - evaluate any loans you have, their rates and terms. Have they been responsive when you required service?

- Accountant - have they been timely responding to you with requests? Are their bills reasonable? Are they providing the services needed? Are they keeping you abreast of changes in the law that impact you or your practice?

- Consultant – how are your ancillary investments performing? Have your business advisors performed a check to ensure their fees are within the market? Are you getting the K-1 tax information (this is your profit or loss from the venture that is reported to the I.R.S.) in a timely basis so you can file your year-end taxes?

- Financial Advisor – if you use a wealth manager, have a meeting each quarter and discuss your investment plan. Your business advisor can facilitate and help you evaluate. Again, as stated above and discussed in detail later, a wealth manager/financial advisor can provide assistance with estate planning, making sure you are staying the course and making regular contributions to your portfolio, discuss rebalancing your portfolio if needed and the pros and cons of rebalancing, educate you on changes that pertain to contributions or tax law changes impacting your portfolio, evaluate outside investments in conjunction with your business advisor, accountant and lawyer, and advise on insurance, and dependents. Once again, note that we advise that the wealth manager be paid an hourly fee to give advice on your entire financial portfolio and not be engaged to pick stocks, mutual funds, or fixed income investments due to the overwhelming data showing that investment professionals cannot identify investments that will beat the basic indexes or the long run particularly after adjusting for their fees. See <u>Mutual Funds: Stock Picking Managers Versus Index Strategies</u>

- Insurance Agent – ask for a yearly insurance assessment to go through all policies, limits, and premiums. Spot check by having your advisor obtain quotes with competing providers (ex. Auto insurance) to make sure your agent is independently shopping the best prices and underwriters. We recommend an independent brokerage firm that will be able to address your personal insurance needs and business needs. See Insurance below for a list of recommended coverages.

CONCEPT 8: Build your Tribe of advisors to protect your interests and remember that alignment of incentives is the key, particularly with your Tribe. Maintain a system of checks and balances with your Tribe, but this is a relationship (as with most things), and paying your advisors fairly and having them working with you for a common goal, mitigates problems for you in the future. Your Tribe protects you so choose good ones, stay close with them, and bond with them.

SUMMARY:

Let's summarize up to this point. You realize that the game of life is a team sport, and interacting and connecting with people is essential to success, so you nurture your internal tribe and recognize their importance. They, in turn, assist you building and maintaining your practice. Furthermore, you've learned the revenue cycle process and put in place systems to ensure that you are efficient and compliant. Since you realize that many of these revenue cycle, legal and accounting issues are beyond your expertise (but not your intelligence) due to having little or no experience or background in these areas, you have built an External Tribe made up of advisors who maintain your best interests. You have taken the steps to establish a system of checks and balances to ensure it. Using these lessons learned, your practice is now functioning well with a system of checks and balances and necessary protections.

Therefore, it is time to begin the process of understanding the money game and how money works for you, rather than you working for it.

Chapter VI
Foundations of Personal Finance

To establish the foundation of personal finance and truly understand money, the first thing to know is that even if you are a sole practitioner, you have a partner, and that partner is the government who takes 30% to 50% of your income.

Taxes - How the Tax System Works

In the United States, the federal tax system is graduated whereby the more money you make, the more you are taxed on the last dollar that you make. Put another way, it is known as a *progressive tax system*, meaning people with higher taxable income pay higher federal income tax rates and people with lower taxable incomes are subject to lower federal income tax rates. This is done by separating or dividing your taxable *Ordinary Income* (the income that is taxed such as wages) into tax brackets. Each tax bracket gets taxed at the corresponding tax rate. Currently, those brackets are: 10%, 12%, 22%, 24%, 32%, 35%, and 37%.

Chapter 6 - Foundations of Personal Finance

The way this works is that in 2022, for example, as a single filer, the first $10,275 you make is taxed at 10%, then your income between $10,276 to $41,775 is taxed at 12%, and so forth. This continues up to 37% for any income over $539,901. So, for someone earning $40,000 per year, he or she is taxed $1,027.50 (10% of $10,275) plus $3,567.00 which is 12% of $29,725 ($40,000 - $10,275).

There are two definitions that are pertinent: *Marginal Tax Rate and Effective Tax Rate*. Your marginal tax rate is the rate you are taxed on the last dollar earned. In the simple example above, your marginal tax rate is 12% since that is the rate on the last dollar earned. However, your effective tax rate is the total tax you pay divided by your income. In the example, it is ($1,027.50 + $3,567.00)/$40,000.00 or 11.48%. The beauty of this is that no matter which bracket you're in, you won't pay that tax rate on your entire income. This is the idea behind the concept of an effective tax rate.

There are other taxes that must be paid. These include the wage-based taxes.

FICA (Federal Insurance Contributions Act) – This tax is deducted from each paycheck. FICA taxes earn credits for Social Security benefits and are tied to the taxpayer's social security number. Every employee including those self-employed is subject to FICA. Similarly, the employer must match the amount paid which is 6.20% of income up to $142,800 as of 2021. For example, a physician making $200,000 is employed by a health system. That physician must pay $8,853.60 (6.20% of $142,800) as his or her FICA contribution, and the health system must match that $8,853.60.

Medicare Tax – This is also known as the "hospital insurance tax," and is a federal employment tax that funds a portion of the Medicare insurance program. Like Social Security tax, Medicare tax is withheld from an employee's paycheck or paid as a self-employment tax. Like FICA, for any wages earned, the employer must withhold 1.45% of taxable income and must then match that 1.45%. There is no cap on the Medicare tax and for higher earners, there is an additional 0.09% tax.

State Unemployment Tax – These taxes fund unemployment programs and pay out benefits to employees who lose their jobs through no fault of their own. This varies by state but is generally paid by the employer. There are exceptions and some states require employees to contribute also.

State Income Tax – this varies by state but can be substantial in certain states such as California; however, some states such as Texas and Florida have no state income tax.

Dividend Income and Capital Gains - One of the key tenets of building wealth is generating passive income and there are huge advantages to generating passive income versus ordinary wage-based income (ordinary income). Nearly all passive income qualifies as *Dividend Income*. Dividend income is defined as income paid out of the profits of a business to its owners/stockholders. It is considered income for tax purposes but if the stock in the company or business is held for at least 60 days, the dividends are defined as *Qualified Dividends*. Currently, qualified dividends are taxed at 0%, 15%, or 20%, depending on your income level and tax filing status. If they are not held for the 60-day holding period, the dividends are considered ordinary (non-qualified) dividends, and taxable distributions are taxed at your marginal income tax rate (up to 37%), which is determined by your taxable earnings.

Similar to dividend income is *Capital Gains*. Capital gains occur when you sell an asset for more than you paid for it. If you hold an investment for more than a year before selling, your profit is typically considered a long-term gain and is taxed at a rate dependent on your income between 0-20%. For example, you purchase a business and sell it a year later for a $100,000 profit. The profit is taxed at the capital gains rate and not your ordinary income rate.

In summary, you pay only <u>half the tax</u> on the passive income generated from your investments. This is why generating passive dividend income is a major point of emphasis and how you build real wealth.

The Mechanics of Paying Taxes

FICA and Medicare tax are withheld from your wages as an employee or self-employed individuals up to their limits (see above) automatically. In 2021, this equates to 7.65% of wages up to $142,800 collectively (6.20% FICA and 1.45% Medicare) plus 1.45% Medicare tax for any wages over $142,800.

You must estimate your federal taxes and state taxes. This is called withholding and is based on what you estimate to be your *Effective Tax Rate*, the average rate that you pay for every dollar earned. We used an example above where the effective rate is 11.48% for a person with $40,000 of taxable income. Note that this is federal tax only and not FICA, Medicare, or state tax.

A better example that is more applicable is a physician single filer who earns $200,000 in reportable taxable employment income. The breakdown using 2021 tax rates is as follows:

FICA (the capped income wage base $142,800 x 6.20%) =	$8,853.60
Medicare ($200,000 taxable income x 1.45%) =	$2,900.00
State Unemployment (employer pays) =	$0.00
Federal Tax Withholding ($33,603 + 32% of the amount over $164,925) =	$44,827.00[3]
State Tax Withholding (example Alabama tax rate is 5%) =	$10,000.00
Total	$66,580.60

---

[3] Note that rather than calculating the amount for each bracket (10%, 12% etc.) this is calculated using tax tables that are readily available on IRS.GOV and figuring the federal tax for a taxpayer with income of $200,000.

Thus, in this example, the physician pays an overall effective rate of 33.29% which is $66,580.60/200,000.00 and should estimate/withhold 5% for state income taxes and about 25% for federal since the 7.65% FICA and Medicare are automatically deducted just to be sure that he or she is not underpaying and subjecting themselves to a penalty.

In the above example, the physician's salary was a set $200,000. However, if the taxable income for the physician varies it should be noted that for every dollar made over $200,000, the physician is paying 32% in federal taxes or more if he or she moves up to a higher tax bracket plus 5% state income tax, so this example works best if the salary is fairly set. If the physician is part of a group or group practice that divides profits (see Division of Profits above), it is likely that they will take a salary in the $200,000 range and then pay themselves a bonus or dividend based on the profits of the practice. In this instance if this taxable income is substantial enough, they must make estimated quarterly payments or be subjected to penalties. A final example of this concept: an orthopedic surgeon estimates that she will make $700,000 in 2021. She will take a salary of $200,000 and withhold 37% for federal taxes even though she realizes that her *effective tax rate* for the $700,000 may be more like 35% but she wants to be sure and not be penalized. She also withholds 5% for state income taxes. For the $500,000 of income beyond her salary that she expects to receive, she must make estimated payments to the IRS (federal) and the State of Alabama and will consult with her accountant who will likely suggest that she withhold and pay 37% of $125,000 ($500,000 divided by 4 quarters) each quarter as federal estimated taxes and 5% of $125,000 each quarter to Alabama to estimate her total year end taxes. When the physician files her returns, the withholding will be credited, and any overpayments will be refunded to her. It is generally better to over withhold rather than under withhold due to very high penalties that the IRS levies on under withholding.

In summary, paying your taxes is an obligation and the law. While there are legal and compliant ways to reduce your taxes through qualified deductions that your accountant will assist you with as part of your Tribe, the core concept of this chapter is for you to understand how the tax system works since this is an area that you must learn and understand to become financially literate.

Chapter VII
Personal Finance

Personal finance is about money - how you handle it and how you handle debt. What does money do? It buys you things of course and it's essential, but *what money really does is it buys you time and freedom and control over your life and decisions.*

The real goal is to make money work for you. How? The objective is to be Balance Sheet Affluent, not Income Statement Affluent by limiting debt, spending less than you make, and becoming a dedicated, patient, and smart investor and allow the magic of compound interest over time to work for you.

However, personal finance is more than just investing. We will discuss investing in depth, but personal finance is also Insurance, Wills and Trusts, Education Planning, Capital Reserves, Retirement Planning and Debt Management. Important questions to ask include:

- How much debt do you have and how is it structured?
- Do you have a Will? Do you need a Trust? How do Trusts and Wills work?

- What will happen upon your Death or if you become Disabled?

- What is your plan for your kid's education?

- What is your plan for Retirement?

- Do you have an emergency fund and how much should it be?

Balance Sheet Rich

As stated above, the goal is to be Balance Sheet Rich, not Income Statement Rich.

What does this mean? If you are balance sheet affluent, it means that you have acquired assets that far exceed your debts and liabilities. Your balance sheet calculates your net worth by adding assets such as your savings, investments such as stocks, bonds, real estate, mutual funds, and other investments plus your home equity minus your debt such as car loans, student loans, credit card debt, etc. According to the United States Census Bureau, the median net worth of Americans in 2020 was $121,700. The goal is for you to accumulate a net worth well in excess of this amount so that you are free from financial concerns and can pursue your life's ambitions, spend time with your family and take care of your patients without unneeded stress.

Why is balance sheet affluence the goal? There are three primary reasons:

1) Balance sheet assets create *Passive Income* - earnings derived from a rental property, dividends from investments, dividends from stocks and bonds or other enterprises in which a person is not actively involved. A common name for passive income is "mailbox money" or money you make while sitting on the beach or playing golf. True wealth is achieved when you generate enough passive income to sustain your lifestyle.

2) Assets that generate passive income and are not spent, compound over time and avail themselves to the "magic" of compound interest.

3) Passive Income tax rates are about half ordinary income rates. This is why the rich get richer. See Taxes.

Compound Interest

Albert Einstein once described compound interest as the "eighth wonder of the world," saying, "he who understands it, earns it; he who doesn't, pays for it" so this is probably the best time to discuss the concept of *compound interest*. According to the website, Investopedia, compound interest (or compounding interest) is the interest on a loan or deposit calculated based on both the initial principal and the accumulated interest from previous periods. Thought to have originated in 17th-century Italy, compound interest can be thought of as "interest on interest," and will make a sum grow at a faster rate than *simple interest*, which is calculated only on the principal amount.

The following is a simple example: When you deposit money in a savings account or a similar account, you'll usually receive interest based on the amount that you deposit. For example, if you deposit $1,000 in an account that pays 1.0 percent annual interest, you'd get $10 in interest after a year. However, compound interest is interest that you earn on interest. So, in the above example, in year 2, you'd earn 1.0 percent on $1,010, or $10.10 in interest payouts. Compound interest accelerates your interest earnings, helping your savings grow more quickly. As time passes, you'll earn interest on ever-larger account balances that have grown with the help of interest earned in prior years. Over the long term, compound interest can cause your interest earnings to snowball very quickly and help you build wealth. In fact, Warren Buffet, the famous investor, said that "compound interest is an investor's best friend" and compared building wealth through interest to rolling a snowball down a hill.

Compound Interest and The Rule of 72

To illustrate the "snowball effect" of compound interest, *The Rule of 72* applies. It is a simple way to determine how long an investment will take to double given a fixed annual rate of interest. It is expressed as a fraction with 72 always being a constant numerator, and the denominator being the compounded rate of return. For example, the Rule of 72 states that $100 invested at an annual fixed interest rate of 9.0% would about take 8 years (72 is the constant/9 is the interest rate) to grow to $200.

Pay Yourself First

If there is only one concept you take away from this book it is to "Pay Yourself First." This means that you automatically invest 10% to 20% of your take home pay into low cost, indexed mutual funds (explained below) that encompass the broad market and harness the power of compound interest to build wealth. We can call this your *Investment Plan*. You auto invest so that it becomes part of your monthly expenses, so you are not tempted to skip a month or try to time the market, or worse increase your spending at the expense of your investment plan. Never deviate from this strategy.

> CONCEPT 9: The building block of acquiring wealth is being a committed investor and investing by growing your balance sheet and accelerating the power of compounding. Pay Yourself First and invest smartly every month without exception. The price of success is high, but so are the rewards.

The Spending Pitfall - What Most People Do

The opposite of acquiring assets and being balance sheet affluent is the concept of income statement rich but balance sheet poor. This what most people do - they spend everything they make. A descriptive and favorite name for this is: "Big Hat, No Cattle." Certainly, you must generate income to become balance sheet rich; however, the distinction between those who are balance sheet rich and those who are income statement rich is that the balance sheet affluent are compulsive savers and careful investors who harness the power of compounding, and the high earning income-statement-set spend excessively.

Do not be seduced by appearances. Many times, those with the largest houses, the most expensive clothes and the most expensive cars are struggling to make their payments every month. They are debt ridden and have no chance to accumulate wealth because they spend everything they make. This is a very common problem amongst physicians and something we see regularly. The lesson is that making a high income is not a guarantee of wealth. The trick is to use that income to make money work for you.

Thomas J. Stanley, Ph.D. is his book The Millionaire Next Door describes both categories very well. Those who spend everything or nearly everything they make are called Under Accumulators of Wealth or UAWs. Those who are balance sheet affluent, the top 25% accumulators of wealth in the U.S., are defined as Prodigious Accumulators of Wealth, or PAWs. Dr. Stanley conducted a study of the affluent and found the following habits of those who are balance sheet affluent or PAWs:

- They live well below their means.

- They allocate their time, energy, and money in ways conducive to building wealth.

- They believe financial autonomy is more important than displaying high social status.

- Their parents did not provide economic outpatient care.
- Their adult children are economically self-sufficient.
- They are proficient in targeting market opportunities.
- They chose the right occupation.

The following are a few thoughts to expand on Dr. Stanley's findings:

- Those who live well below their means are not living like paupers. In fact, his study concluded that the balance sheet affluent live in very nice houses and have a very comfortable lifestyle. However, the distinguishing factor is that they simply save between 10% to 20% or perhaps more of their tax home pay.

- Allocating time and energy to building wealth is harnessing the power of compound interest by investing wisely.

- PAWs drive very nice cars but very few will spend more than $150,000 for an automobile even if they can afford it. They would rather drive a $90,000 Lexus and invest the difference.

- They raise their children with the expectation that they must have a career and be economically self-sufficient and not expect to live off the family wealth.

- They raise their children to understand how to control money and not spend everything they make so that when the children become adults, they are economically self-sufficient.

- Regarding opportunities, for a physician this could mean opening a new office in a growing community. Your practice is your biggest asset in many ways because it generates the income that allows you to invest and accumulate wealth. The practice of medicine is what you know best, so investing in yourself and in something you can control provides the best chance for success.

- Medicine is a wonderful, rewarding, and noble profession. It statistically is a high-income profession but what matters is what you do with the income after you pay the tax man.

Remember, the rich buy assets (items that appreciate) and avail themselves to the compounding of those assets and everyone else buys liabilities (items that depreciate).

> CONCEPT 10: Buy assets, not liabilities.

The Millionaire Next Door Wealth Formula

Dr. Stanley defines PAWs objectively by using a formula.: Multiply your age x 10% and then multiply that by your pretax annual household income from all sources except inheritances. This, less any inherited wealth, is what your net worth should be. The goal is to be 2X expected net worth. This is a good goal but be aware that when you start your career it is difficult to meet this benchmark. However, if you follow a prescribed and careful investment and personal finance plan, in a few years you should have no trouble meeting or exceeding this standard.

Example

Dr. A is 41 years old and makes $155,000 a year. He would multiply 41 x 10% to equal 4.1. Then he multiplies 4.1 times his pretax income as follows: 4.1 x $155,000 = $635,500. Thus, his net worth should be $635,500 but to be an over accumulator of wealth or PAW, it should be 2x the expected net worth or $635,500 x 2 = $1,271,000.

The Expectation Trap: Physicians and Common Barriers to Wealth Accumulation

In 2020, a physician's average salary was $243,000 and in 2019, a dentist's average salary was $155,600. On average, doctors earn more than 4x the income of the average American household. The Millionaire Next Door research found that physicians typically aren't good at accumulating wealth. For every one doctor in the PAW group, there were two in the UAW category. Why are so many physicians UAWs? One of the reasons is a late start. After four years of college, four years of medical school and several years of residency, they graduate, and play catch up. Another reason which ties in to the one above is something that personal finance author Dave Ramsey calls "Doc-itis.". It all has to do with the sacrifice and delay society places on living the good life. Society believes that doctors are expected to: live in an expensive home, dress in style, drive expensive vehicles.

Chapter 7 - Personal Finance

If you live in a modest home and drive a four-year-old Honda, many assume that the physicians practice is mediocre. These expectations along with the time sacrificing in school and residency while their peers are earning and purchasing facilitates hyper consumption.

A balanced approach to this is recommended. You do not have to live like a pauper to accumulate wealth and build passive income. The reality is far from it. Rather, once you start earning disposable income, develop a personal financial plan and that includes purchasing a few coveted luxury items. The key, of course, is following your Investment Plan (10% to 20% invested every month) and sticking with that plan.

A final example is illustrative. In Texas, there is no state income tax, but they make up for it with high property taxes. University Park is a suburb of Dallas and is considered one of its best neighborhoods. In fact, Dr. Stanley used the University Park zip code as one of the zip codes in his study for The Millionaire Next Door. For our purposes, Dr. C purchases a 4-bedroom, 3,000 square foot house in University Park, he pays $1,500,000, the average price today. This a modernly equipped house in a great neighborhood with public schools that are consistently in the top rankings in Texas. Each year he will pay approximately $30,000 in property taxes. Dr. C is not living like a pauper by any means in one of the nicest neighborhoods in Texas. However, his colleague Dr. K who makes approximately the same income as Dr. C purchases a 5,000 square foot house in University Park for $2,800,000 and pays $56,000 per year in property taxes and approximately an extra $4,000 per year in additional utilities and maintenance on the house. Over twenty years, the average time a family raises kids and keeps a large house, Dr. C will have nearly $1,700,000[4] by investing the additional $2,500 per month that he saves in taxes by not purchasing the extra-large house. Also, this does not take into the account the difference in mortgage payments he saves and could invest since stocks tend to appreciate faster than residential real estate over the long run.

---

[4] $2,500 per month over 20 years at a compounded rate of 9.0%.

Accumulating wealth is not about constant financial sacrifice and sacrificing nice things or living in below average neighborhoods, it's about making wise choices, creating excess cash flow and investing that excess cash flow to allow it to snowball and grow over time.

> CONCEPT 11: The key to being wealthy is very simple, yet sometimes hard to grasp: 1) don't spend everything you make - Pay Yourself First by automatically investing 10% to 20% of your after tax income, 2) commit to investing for the long-run in low cost investments that diversify your portfolio such as an index mutual funds tracking the S&P 500, Wilshire 5000 and the bond market, 3) control and limit your debt, 4) be rationale, turn off CNBC and understand that fluctuations in the market are normal, 5) play the long game, stay the course with your consistent investment plan and let the "magic" of compound interest work for you.

Developing a Personal Financial Plan

If you follow Concept 9 and particularly save 10% to 20% or more of your take home pay and invest those monies in low cost indexed mutual funds without deviating from your investment plan, you will be well on your way to accumulating wealth and achieving financial freedom over time. In fact, if do nothing else, you should achieve financial independence by the end of your career or sooner.

However, there are still critical steps to augment your finances and there are landmines along the way that must be recognized. Playing good defense is about keeping your money and using it to build wealth. In order to do this, you must have a personal financial plan and stay with that plan; thus, this section is set forth in chronological order to assist you constructing your own personal financial plan.

Constructing a Personal Financial Plan.

Debt. Debt is the first issue to address. **You cannot obtain real wealth with excessive debt.** The goal is to have no debt. However, for those starting their careers that goal may be impractical in the short term. So if you have debt, there is good debt and bad debt. *Good debt* is used to further create income and wealth. A great example are student loans. Student loans allow you to pursue your medical degree and, in turn, engender higher than average income. A business loan to start up your business or grow your business is good debt. A working capital line of credit to assist with temporary cash flow is also considered good debt. For temporary cash flow and to keep from keeping excess cash on hand that could be invested, a working capital line of credit is highly recommended particularly if you do not draw down on it; however, if you must use your line of credit, pay it off as soon as possible since it's your backup or reserve and the goal is to be debt free. See <u>Cash Reserves</u> below. Traditionally, a mortgage is considered good debt with the caveat that the size of the mortgage does not require you to deviate you from your investment plan of saving at least 10% to 20% of your take home pay. In sum, student loans, a business loan, a working capital line of credit and a mortgage are the only good debt you should have.

Bad debt is more problematic. UAWs have bad debt. This is debt used to purchase depreciating items. Do not use debt to purchase depreciating items. Debt should be used as temporary assistance to increase your net worth.

The worst debt is credit card debt, and it must be addressed first due to high interest.[5] This includes the major bank cards such as Mastercard and Visa as well as department store cards. Credit card debt is so insidious because it compounds at a rate of up to 24%. You must eliminate all credit card debt immediately because it will be an anchor to your quest for financial independence. If you have credit card debt, cut your spending, and use the savings to pay this debt off completely. If that is not possible currently, tear up all but one card for emergency purposes and work with your banker to consolidate into one loan at a lower interest rate and then pay this loan off as soon as your income improves. This is first and foremost.

There is hybrid debt that is likely bad debt but may not be avoidable. Automobile loans fall into this category. A discussion regarding how to purchase an automobile is later in this chapter but having no car loan is preferred. If you do have a car loan, look for a subsidized loan by the manufacturer. Typically, these are well below bank loans and are offered as an inducement to purchase the car. Home equity loans are loans against the equity in your home that can be used for just about anything. Home improvement is common and that is why this type of loan could be characterized as good debt **if** it truly improves the value of your house; however, home equity loans are expensive and should typically be avoided. Home improvement can normally be funded out of cash reserves and finally note that outdoor living areas and pools are very nice but may not actually add value.

Should you pay off your student loan early? This is the most common question asked in my class. My view is that your goal is to eventually be debt free and thus, you should pay off your student

---

[5] Actually, pawnbroker loans, payroll loans and auto title loans are the worst debt due to extremely high interest rates, but for purposes of this book, it is assumed that avoiding that type of financing is obvious.

debt as soon as possible but not at the expense of foregoing your investment plan due to the above-described snowball effect of compounding interest. The building block of wealth is saving 10% to 20% or more of your paycheck and investing it in low-cost index funds. You can then use any excess after paying your reasonable living expenses to accelerate and pay off debt. It will give you peace of mind and make you less vulnerable when economic conditions change.

As stated above, with certain exceptions described below, debt is an anchor and an impediment to wealth. A common argument in favor of keeping debt is if the interest rate on a loan is well below the expected stock market return for the S&P 500 of 10% per annum, it is better to keep the debt and use the money saved to invest. While there is merit to this argument, this is a personal choice and it only pertains to the three types of debt that are recommended – Student Loans, Home Mortgages and Auto Loans.[6] It is encouraged to eliminate as much debt as possible and this includes accelerating *good debt* payments such as car loans, student loans and home mortgages. If you do choose to keep debt, subsidized car loans at absurdly low rates such as 1.9% to 2.9%, and mortgages below 6% are acceptable debt and may provide some tax advantages.

In summary, for someone just starting their career, it is not practical to be debt free. That is the goal to work toward. Eliminate all but the *good debt* and try to accelerate payments on that debt as long as you Pay Yourself First and save and invest 10% to 20% or more of your tax home pay.

Cash Reserves. There is a prevalent theory that you should keep 6 months cash for personal expenses on hand. I feel that this is impractical and results in an investor having excess cash on hand that could be used for investments. Rather, it is suggested that 45 to

---

[6] A business loan and line of credit are short term loans and are to be paid off quickly. The only long term (> 1year) debt recommended are student loans, home mortgages and perhaps auto loans.

60 days of cash reserves be kept to cover monthly expenses and a $100,000 line of credit be set up with your banker (tribe member) that can be drawn upon in the event of an emergency. The cost to maintain a line of credit is nominal and much more practical as an emergency reserve.

Purchasing a Home. Purchasing a home may be the largest purchase you will make in your lifetime. Be sure you are not overextending yourself and maintain the ability to save and invest (Pay Yourself First). You don't want to be house rich and cash poor. While the housing market is appreciating rapidly at the time that this is written, houses generally do appreciate but typical appreciation of real estate (residential) underperforms the stock market as defined as the S&P 500 in the long run. Also, note that your home is a cost center, and it is expensive to maintain. As noted in the example earlier, the larger the house, the higher the cost to maintain (property taxes, utilities, general maintenance). Finally, you must live somewhere and purchasing a home provides stability and emotional piece of mind. However, choose wisely since not all homes and neighborhoods are alike. Neighborhoods that have maintained their value over a long period of time and have schools that are highly ranked are typically the most expensive, but also many times provide for the best appreciation.

Should you purchase a house during residency? Note that brokerage commissions are typically 6% plus closing fees are close to 1%. Thus, when you purchase your house, it is worth 93% of what you paid for it. Put another way, it must appreciate by 7.5% before you recoup your investment. If you plan to be in the house over three years, it may make sense to purchase your home, but if you are unsure or know you will be in that location no more than 2 to 3 years, renting may make sense.

Should you build or purchase an existing home? While there are caveats to this, purchasing an existing home typically is the wise financial decision. Certainly, older homes require maintenance and may not have all the modern accoutrements but many of the costs (builder profit, real estate fees, design fees) are absorbed by the original owner(s).

How much can you afford to pay? Deciding how much you can afford and how to structure your home loan presents another challenge to your financial plan. It is recommended that you get pre-qualified for a mortgage using a mortgage broker selected by your real estate agent or business advisor. Being pre-qualified allows you to move fast on market opportunities and perhaps reduce the price of the house you purchase by offering to close fast if the seller accepts your offer. Remember that the core to building wealth is investing 10% to 20% or more of your after-tax income in low-cost index mutual funds. Therefore, back into what you can afford by determining your income after taxes, subtract living expenses other than house expenses and the difference will give you what you can afford to pay each month in housing expenses. However, you must factor in property taxes, increased utilities if you are moving to a larger house, repairs, and maintenance. Typically, you do not want to spend more than 25% of your tax home pay on housing expenses.

How to best obtain a home loan? Once you determine how much you can pay each month, as suggested above, work with an independent mortgage broker to find a loan that meets your needs. An independent broker will shop the market for home lenders, and this is recommended rather than using your bank since they may offer only one or two products. You can compare the brokers recommendation with your bank and decide which one fits your needs. Use your business advisor or accountant to assist if needed. As a physician there are programs offered by banks that do not require a down payment. Those could be good programs if you are not required to pay PMI (Purchase Mortgage Insurance) or insurance that a bank requires the lender to pay if they do not put at least 20% up as a down payment.

What time length for the mortgage and should it be fixed or variable rate? If you purchase a $500,000 home and enter into a 30-year fixed rate mortgage at 4%, you will pay a total of $359,348 in interest payments over the term of the loan or 72% of the purchase price in interest. Contrast this with a 15-year mortgage at the same rate. You will pay only $165,719 in interest over the term of that loan or about 33% of the purchase price. Therefore, it is suggested that accelerating debt payments is a good thing. However, it is not necessarily recommended to obtain a 15-year mortgage; rather, a 30-year mortgage gives flexibility especially when starting a career and particularly with the expectation that your income will rise. A 30-year mortgage has lower payments and give you the choice to accelerate payments whereas a 15-year mortgage requires higher payments each month. You can turn your 30-year mortgage into a 15 year as your cash flow increases. The key is to make sure that your mortgage has no prepayment penalty and allows you to make additional payments so you can accelerate paying off the debt once you have excess cash. Again, once you are paying yourself first and following your investment plan and still have excess cash, there is that tradeoff between using that excess cash to accelerate payments on a low-cost mortgage at 4% or using that same money to invest with an expected historical return of 9%-10% percent. Home mortgage is *good debt* and the last debt to pay off because of currently low interest rates and the tax advantages of maintaining a mortgage since homeowners who itemize their tax returns can deduct property taxes they pay on their main residence and interest payments. There are income phase out restrictions so consult with your accountant, but again, this is a personal decision and the benefit, stability, and peace of mind of being debt free are something that should be weighed.

Once approved for a loan, you can shop in your preferred neighborhood and purchase at a favorable price particularly if there are similar homes in the area and the seller is motivated. This means making offers perhaps 5% to 8% below the asking price for a house. You may be surprised when the seller accepts your reasonably discounted offer[7]. This is a good use of your business advisor who can help you with this process also.

---

[7] Market conditions apply but a reasonable low offer is recommended, not a lowball offer that will waste everyone's time. Remember you must understand how everyone in a transaction gets paid and, in this instance, your real estate agent is paid on the price paid for the house and may be a little more reticent so encourage your agent to negotiate the way you want. A good real estate agent wants to sell the house and will understand your strategy as long as your discounted offers are reasonable.

Purchase a home in a stable neighborhood that you can afford and will not disrupt your personal investment plan so you always Pay Yourself First. Shop different mortgages using an independent broker, negotiate the price, accelerate mortgage payments after you pay off your other debt. In sum, don't be house rich and cash poor.

Purchasing a Car. Earlier in this chapter, good debt and bad debt was discussed with the emphasis on limiting debt as much as possible and only having *good debt* (the debt you use to assist you in growing your income and wealth) such as student loans and temporary business loans. All these loans, with possibly the exception of a home mortgage, should be paid off as soon as possible as long as you are saving and investing 10% to 20% of your after tax take home pay first since that is the priority.

Car loans fall into a separate category because they are typically necessary but are not *good debt* because cars depreciate or lessen in value. Remember the mantra, buy assets (appreciating items), not liabilities. However, you must make purchases for living expenses such as transportation, and traditionally coming up with the entire amount to purchase car is a challenge.

Regarding cars, the best advice is to purchase an affordable car and drive it for as long as it is safe and reliable. For example, you purchase a $45,000 Infiniti and drive it for 7 years and then sell it for $17,000[8]. The cost of the Infiniti (exclusive of maintenance and insurance) is $28,000, or only $4,000 per year. However, by contrast, you purchase the same Infiniti and trade it after 2 years. The forecasted depreciation on that car is 32% or $14,400 or $7,200 per year. Therefore, it costs you almost twice as much if you trade frequently. For the example, Infiniti's have tended to hold their value better than the average automobile. A better example is a 2021 Cadillac Escalade costing $87,500 that loses 30% in 2 years, or over $13,000 per year. Finally, the above examples assumed a new car purchase. A better strategy is to purchase a used automobile and let the original owner

---

[8] Source: www.autopadre.com

take the initial hit in depreciation because cars depreciate rapidly the first three years and then after year three, they still depreciate but at a much slower rate. Certified used vehicles generally have an extended warranty and are a good choice.

Now that the "correct" financial strategy for automobile purchases is highlighted let's be a little more practical. We realize that cars are very important to some and driving a 10-year-old Honda is not necessarily practical or desirable. You need to have some fun and life is meant to be enjoyed. Therefore, the following are the steps recommended for purchasing a car:

- Determine which car you want to purchase. Note that some depreciate more than others and you can use sites such as www.autopadre to gather this information; e.g., a Maserati depreciates much faster than a Lexus.

- Check reliability to ensure that the car is not being recalled or has major mechanical issues. This is an easy internet search.

- Leasing v. Buying – unless there are substantial manufacturer subsidies, leasing is more expensive than buying because:

    o New cars are leased, and they depreciate faster than used cars because you are paying for the car during the time when it most rapidly depreciates. See above.

    o Leasing can be confusing, and it is hard to determine the actual interest rate you are paying because there are actually two payments: 1) the principal and interest on the difference between the purchase price and depreciated value at the end the lease term (how much it depreciated); and 2) interest on the residual value of the car.

    o If you lease one car after another, monthly payments go on forever and you are on the debt train. By contrast, as discussed, the longer you keep a vehicle after the loan is paid off, the more value you get out of it.

- o Leasing is a way to get into a more expensive vehicle for lower monthly payments. Again, it is debt and not necessarily good debt.

- Negotiate the purchase price. Depending on market conditions, 7% below asking price is a good goal. Your business advisor can assist if needed.

  - o As part of negotiating the price, use sites such as www.cars.com or www.autotrader.com to find the car you want and negotiate with the different dealers to get it at the best price. Competition is good so use it to your advantage.

- Look for subsidized offers at low interest rates as long as the car that is being subsidized is not a high depreciating vehicle due to its expected value or a newer model coming out which also lowers it future value. You could get a great loan but be stuck with a car that will cost you more in the long run.

In summary, as long as you are sticking with your investment plan (Pay Yourself First), you can drive a nice car if the car you drive is important to you. Try to purchase used and look for a certified pre-owned if possible because, as stated above, they typically have an extended warranty. Note that higher end automobiles are very expensive to fix after the warranty runs. Do your research and make sure that the car has a good reliability record and a reasonable depreciation rate. Negotiate the price by shopping around your region and avoid leasing if possible.

Boats and Planes. Unless your passion is fishing, sailing, or boating, or you can't live a happy life without flying yourself, there is one thing to say about planes and boats: If it floats or flies, it is generally better to rent it.

Personal Insurance. Insurance is essentially a means of protection from financial loss. It is a form of risk management, primarily used to hedge against the risk of a contingent or uncertain loss. An entity which provides insurance is known as an insurer, an insurance company, an insurance carrier, or an underwriter.

What insurance do I need? At a minimum:

- Major Medical Insurance
- Property and Casualty Insurance (auto, homeowners, personal liability/umbrella)
- Life Insurance (term or whole life)
- Disability Income Insurance
- Long Term Care Insurance

Major Medical Insurance – it goes without saying that you and your family should have major medical insurance to cover health and dental and vision. Employers offer this insurance, and it is mandated for large employers as part of the Affordable Care Act (ACA). For those in a group practice there are other options including the ACA exchanges, and plans offered through traditional insurance companies sold through brokers.

Health Savings Accounts (HSAs) are another option. They are like personal savings accounts, but the money in them is used to pay for health care expenses. A key benefit is the money you deposit in your HSA is not taxed. To be eligible, the HSA requires individuals to first have a high deductible health insurance plan. A high deductible plan requires you to first spend at least $1,400 for an individual and $2,800 for a family on health-related costs before the HSA funds can be used. The HSA account is funded with pre-tax dollars and the contribution limits per year are $3,600 for individuals and $7,200 for families. Any funds in the plan at the end of the year can be rolled over to the next year indefinitely.

Shopping health insurance is wise because it is one of your largest annual expenses. If you are not employed and utilizing the health insurance offered by your employer, it is suggested that you contact your payroll and human resources company that you use for your employees as well as your insurance broker.

Property and Casualty Insurance - home and auto insurance are also necessary, of course, and typically required by a financial institution providing your financing; understanding the type of coverage is important. The word "casualty" is a term used to describe your liability to others. In the personal insurance market, you will find most of the time, your casualty and property insurance combined in one policy. Property insurance, commonly called Homeowners insurance, covers your residence structure and your contents (anywhere in the world), it is important to make sure that you have enough coverage to replace your property in the event of a loss. Building costs rise annually so be sure that you review the amount of your coverage annually. Additional coverages to consider for your home and contents are 1) wind insurance which is generally included in your Homeowner's policy automatically unless you live in an area prone to wind related weather and 2) flood insurance which is traditionally an extra policy in your insurance coverage. Finally, many times an insurer will have a wind policy that differs from your flood policy. It is important to understand that if there is a claim, the insurance companies will try to deny the claim and assert that the damage is due to flood if it is the wind insurer and vice versa. If possible, you want the same company covering both wind and flood. Again, ask your insurance agent/broker should assist you with coverage decisions.

For personal auto insurance which encompasses automobiles, trucks, trailers, and with certain insurance companies, other mobile equipment, provides the following are the most common and recommended coverages:

- Comprehensive – this is damage caused by or related to theft, animals (including collision with animals), vandalism and weather. You should think of it as coverage that *doesn't* cover your vehicle colliding with something — that would be handled via collision coverage.

- Collision - Collision coverage protects your car if it collides with another vehicle or fixed object. This coverage applies regardless of fault.

- Gap Insurance – this covers the difference between the amount an insurance company will pay you for your car if it's totaled and the amount you might owe to a lender or dealership. Because most car insurance policies reimburse you based on what they deem the car to be worth at the time of the accident and not replacement cost value, it's possible to end up "underwater" on a car loan or lease, meaning you owe more on your auto loan than the vehicle is worth. This coverage is not automatic and must be added to your policy.

- Bodily Injury and Property Liability – Costs for injuries, death, or damage from an accident you caused.

- Medical Payment Coverage and Personal Injury Protection – they are similar but distinct. Medical Payments (Med Pay) will cover the medical payments for you and your passengers in your vehicle if <u>they are</u> injured in a crash. Personal Injury Protection (PIP) is similar to <u>includes</u> medical payments coverage but also will cover other documented losses such as your lost wages.

- Uninsured/Underinsured – this covers property damage to your vehicle and bodily injury to you or your passengers when the other person (who is at fault) has no insurance or is underinsured.

- Rental Car – this is a cheap and good addition to your policy so be sure that in the event that you have an accident, the insurance company will provide you with a rental car while your car is being repaired or replaced.

Work with your insurance agent/broker on the limits. Each state has minimums but be aware that you are a target as a high-income earner so purchase encompassing coverage.

In addition, an Umbrella policy is an important insurance policy to add to your portfolio. An umbrella policy adds additional liability limits over your home, auto policies and any other personal insurance policy in the event of a catastrophic event when you are deemed liable or if you are sued. An umbrella policy offers liability protection on your property and beyond it. It also serves as backup in case someone files a lawsuit that exceeds the amount of your regular coverage. It is a hedge against lawsuits that are not covered by your other policies. For example, you get into an auto accident with another person, and they sue you for negligent driving, or someone slips in your backyard and claims that they are permanently disabled and sue you for loss of future income and the amount is over and above your insurance limits.

How much umbrella coverage do you need? Many agents/brokers will recommend you protect your current personal net worth or your potential future net worth. If your net worth or your assets exceed the amount of your coverage limits on your auto, home, malpractice policies, then purchase an umbrella policy. These polices are relatively cheap and protect your assets.

Life Insurance - to continue regarding key purchases, the role of life insurance (whole life vs. term) is extremely important. As mentioned in the definition, insurance is a risk management tool. It guards against risk of loss unexpected events and catastrophic loss. Life insurance is a key component of your financial plan because it provides for your dependents upon your demise. The amount to have should be enough insurance to extinguish your debts and provide for your dependents. Note that this amount may change over time so annual meetings with your financial advisor and insurance broker are required. There are essentially two types of life insurance.

- Term is the cheapest and has a finite "term." What this means is that it covers you for a fixed period, such as 20 or 30 years, and pays out if you die during the term. If you outlive the term and your coverage ends, your beneficiaries don't receive the money.

- Whole life is just what it says. It covers you for your entire life and thus is more expensive than term insurance because it includes an additional cost for a cash value feature. It is generally sold as an investment vehicle and the premiums are paid and grow over time. Once you've built up enough cash value, you can borrow against the account, or surrender the policy for cash or allow the policy to continue without payment until the cash value is gone. The term "Universal Life" is also commonly used, while whole life policies guarantee the premium payment regardless of interest rate performance in the marketplace. Universal Life is subject to interest rates in the marketplace and may require a future increase in payment if the market doesn't perform as proposed.

Which is better Term or Whole Life? Term and whole life both have their advantages in certain situations. Generally, term makes sense for most because it is cheaper and addresses early term catastrophic occurrences when your net worth may not be able to pay off your debts or provide long term for your dependents. Term insurance also provides increased coverage for a period of time, for example, term insurance provides a peace of mind for your children's education until they graduate from college. Consider whole life insurance for longer-term financial planning goals such as estate planning, funding a trust or providing for a lifelong dependent since whole life can be one of the vehicles to fund a trust and provide care for that dependent after you are gone. In terms of estate planning, whole life is an excellent estate planning vehicle because it can assist paying for estate taxes that your heirs will be required to pay, hence allowing them to inherit more.[9] A combination of both whole life and term

---

[9] Currently, at the federal level, the top estate tax rate is 40% on any amount over the estate tax exemption. This estate and gift tax exemption of $11,700,000 per individual sunsets in 2025, and the exemption amount will drop back down to the prior law's $5,000,000, which when adjusted for inflation is expected to be about $6,200,000 for an individual or $12,400,000 for married couples. This means that if you are married, the first $12,400,000 of your estate is not taxed but once you and your spouse die, any excess above the $12.4 million is taxed at a top rate of up to 40% as described above. However, there is uncertainty regarding the estate tax exemption amount since Congress is currently proposing changes and either accelerating the sunset provision or lowering the exemption amount. While this amount sounds like it is not applicable to those new in their careers, it is likely an issue if you follow your investment plan and you should consult with your financial advisor (Tribe member) about this each year and plan accordingly. Finally, some states have estate tax laws also and should be factored into your financial plan.

insurance over the course of your life is often a sound strategy to protect your future. As a physician and high-income earner, you will be inundated with insurance brokers wanting to sell you insurance. Typically, they will suggest whole life policies, or the ones paying the highest commission. While the advantages to whole life are discussed above, it is suggested that you be very skeptical regarding the claim that whole life is a good investment. For reasons discussed in detail in the chapter on investments, whole life plans nearly always utilize active management (the manager picks the investments) and those management fees are generally very expensive and nearly impossible to overcome as compared to a simple, passively managed index fund tracking the S&P 500 or Wilshire 5000.

Disability insurance is essential if you get too sick or injured to work. It will be used to care for you and your family as a supplemental income source. Purchase disability insurance to cover your future income, pay your bills and your debts. Some employers will offer short and long-term disability benefits to their employees. A short-term policy helps you immediately after an incident, and a long-term policy helps provide financial protection for disabilities that can last for years. You can also pay for additional coverage on top of the benefits you get at work to help provide extra financial protection. Purchase disability insurance since this a key risk management tool and important part of your financial plan. We suggest you use your insurance broker and financial advisor to determine which disability polices and amounts fit your needs.

Long term care insurance covers nursing-home care, home-health care, and personal or adult daycare for individuals 65 or older or with a chronic or disabling condition that needs constant supervision. It is something worth considering and is very dependent on each individual. This is something to discuss with your financial advisor each year.

Business Insurance – In addition, to personal insurance, you must have business insurance. The most common policies are called Businessowners Policies and include the following coverage:

- General Liability/Hired and Non-Owned – for your business, general liability coverage insures you against any claim that arises from injuries, and property damage on your premises. This is commonly referred to as "slip and fall" coverage. Hired and non-owned provides protection if an employee gets into a wreck off premises but is working at your behest i.e., the employee goes to the bank and has an accident.

- Building and Property – insures against loss for any equipment, furniture, artwork that is damaged onsite but also covers your structure or, as a tenant, your improvements to the structure.

- Business Interruption - Business interruption insurance is a type of insurance that covers the loss of income that a business suffers after a disaster. The income loss covered may be due to disaster-related closing of the business facility or due to the rebuilding process after a disaster. Note this deductible is measured in "hours" rather than a dollar amount.

- Cyber Coverage- protects businesses, and individuals providing services for such businesses, from Internet-based risks, and more generally from risks relating to information technology infrastructure, information privacy, information governance liability, and related activities.

Business coverages that are traditionally not included in a Businessowners policy include:

- Medical Malpractice or Professional Liability - Medical malpractice insurance covers physicians for claims resulting from allegations of wrong site surgery, misdiagnosis, surgical errors, medication errors, childbirth-related injuries, and other claims of wrongdoing. Common exclusions include reckless or intentional conduct, illegal acts, misrepresentation on the application, and sexual misconduct. Each state has its own limits, and you should consult with your attorney and colleagues and then work with a broker specializing in medical malpractice to obtain the policy that is best for you. If you are employed, it is likely that medical malpractice coverage is covered under your employment agreement and is obtained for you as part of the group practice umbrella; however, you must be aware of the limits and may consider purchasing supplemental coverage so you should consult with your business advisor and attorney.

- Employment Practices Coverage (EPL)– covers the judgement and legal expenses when an employee files a lawsuit alleging discrimination, wrongful termination, harassment, or other wrongful acts.

- Workers Compensation Coverage - provides statutory injury and disability/lost wage benefits for your employees injured while working for you. Consider that in addition to being required in most states if you employ 5 or more employees, workers compensation is also a bar against a lawsuit by your employee against you. For this reason, consider purchasing workers compensation coverage even if you have fewer than 5 employees and not required by the state to purchase the coverage.

For personal and business insurance, these are the most common coverages available and at a minimum the ones that are recommended; however, the market is constantly changing as well as each individual's current situation. This highlights the need to obtain sound insurance advice. For this reason, we recommend large insurance brokerage firms who can provide the gamut of services and specialize in several areas. As stated above, you will be inundated with agents/brokers who want to sell you insurance. It is imperative that you use your business advisor or accountant to assist you finding highly specialized insurance agents/brokers who will look at your business and personal situation in its entirety and craft policies that fit your needs. Thus, a final word on insurance and insurance agents/brokers. You must always understand the motivation of those who work on your behalf. There is nothing wrong with having an agent/ broker who earns a commission because that is how they are paid and paying your advisors for excellent service engenders loyalty. As long as you are aware of their motivation, there are excellent insurance brokers who will guide you and steer you into insurance products that fit your specific needs. Again, use your business advisor and accountant or lawyer to help select a broker who will work in your best interests. They are a valuable part of your tribe.

Educational Planning – an important component of financial planning is addressing education for your dependents. The most common vehicle is a 529 Plan which is a tax-advantaged savings account designed to be used for the beneficiary's education expenses. Anyone can open a 529 plan and up to $75,000 ($150,000 per married couple) can be contributed to the plan each year. They allow for after-tax dollars to invest in the plan and any growth is non-taxable if the funds are used for educational expenses including not only tuition, but housing, supplies, computers, food expenses and student loan repayments. Typically, 529 plans are used for college tuition, but you can also use up to $10,000 for K-12 tuition. Also, if you are using a 529 plan to save for college, your savings will have a minimal impact on financial aid eligibility. Finally, anyone can contribute to a 529 plan, and this includes grandparents and relatives.

There are also prepaid tuition plans. Prepaid tuition plans are a type of 529 plan. They allow family members—parents, grandparents, and other relatives—to pay for a student's college tuition at current tuition rates, even if they don't attend college for years. A prepaid tuition program may be used to pay for future college tuition at any of the sponsoring state's eligible colleges or universities. Currently, only nine states offer this option: Florida, Maryland, Massachusetts, Michigan, Mississippi, Nevada, Pennsylvania, Texas, and Washington. If you live in one of these states, your beneficiary must attend an in-state college or university, and you can't use the money to pay for any other expenses. They may also provide a proportional payment for enrollment at private or out-of-state institutions. For this reason, unless you are absolutely sure that your child will attend college in-state, the regular 529 plan is recommended, even though you do not receive the benefit of locking in tuition at current rates, because the flexibility of a regular 529 plan and the ability to pay for other expenses (housing, food etc.) using a regular plan.

How does a 529 plan work? Each state has its own regular 529 plan and it is administered through an investment company and the contributions are held in in mutual funds holding stocks and bonds. The best 529 plans shift the beneficiary from a growth mode in mostly stocks when they are younger to a more conservative portfolio as the beneficiary gets closer to using the funds from the plan. It should be noted that the state that administers the plan doesn't matter, unless you opt for a prepaid plan, because you can use the monies to attend school in any state. Rather, look for low-cost plan with low management fees and no-account maintenance and service fees. Vanguard, Schwab, and Fidelity have low cost 529 plans and they are recommended. Utah, Ohio, Nevada, and Virginia are a few higher performing, low cost 529 plans.

In summary, regarding educational expenses for your children, a regular 529 plan is the best way to save for college (and private school) since it provides tax free growth, and any withdrawals are not taxed as long as the proceeds are used for educational expenses. The regular 529 plan is very flexible and typically a better choice than a prepaid plan. It is recommended that you choose a low-cost plan that automatically adjusts the asset allocation mix as the child nears college age.

Estate Planning – the purpose of an estate plan is to allow your dependents to be protected and live comfortably upon your demise. Everyone should have, at a minimum, an estate plan made up of three components:

1. A Will
2. A Living Will; and
3. A Power of Attorney.

Your attorney should work with you to develop these documents as part of your estate plan.

Who needs a Will? It is suggested that every adult should have a *Will* even if you are single. They are easy and cheap and saves your family time and heartache. A will states who assumes ownership of your assets and belongings after you die. You appoint an Executor in the will to carry out your wishes, such as how to distribute your assets (including life insurance proceeds) and extinguish your liabilities, as well as other personal wishes; e.g., whether you want to be buried or cremated, or who should inherit your favorite watch. If you have children, you use your will to name a guardian for them if you die before they turn age of majority in your state. If you don't write a will, your assets are distributed according to plans outlined in your state's intestacy laws. That is not recommended.

In addition, you should have a *Living Will* or advanced directives. A living will is a legal document in which a person specifies what actions should be taken for their health if they are no longer able to make decisions for themselves because of illness or incapacity. This is important so you can give your loved one's instructions on how you are to be treated in the event of a medical emergency.

What is a Power of Attorney? A *Power of Attorney* document authorizes the person you choose to handle financial matters on your behalf if you are unable for whatever reason. Each state has its own rules regarding power of attorney. You can set a power of attorney up to become active only if you are incapacitated, or you can create it so that it is effective immediately if you want to use it for convenience, such as when you are out of the country. Note the similarity between an executor and a power of attorney, but understand that they are different. An executor administers your financial matters *when you are dead* and is designated in your will, and your designated power of attorney administers *when you are incapacitated*. They can be the same person but are designated in separate documents because they address two separate circumstances.

Advanced Estate Planning - Revocable and Irrevocable Trusts
Another estate planning tool is a trust, and specifically a *Revocable Trust* that is also known as a *Living Trust*. As you accumulate wealth, trusts are a common estate planning instrument. A revocable living trust is kind of a "Will substitute." It is a legal entity created to hold, manage, and distribute your assets and property on your behalf. A trust survives your death and continues in perpetuity. You appoint a *Trustee* who administers your estate after you die subject to your specific wishes. For example, you and your wife appoint each other as co-trustees. When one of you dies, the other is responsible for the estate and then names a successor trustee. Now when your spouse passes, the successor trustee administers the estate and divides the property and assets subject to your wishes. For illustration, you and your wife have $10 million in assets including your home, property, and stocks and bonds. The only debt is a home mortgage. Upon your death, your spouse, as co-trustee, continues as usual and pays the bills and mortgage every month since you specified in the trust that your spouse will continue to live in the same manner that he or she is accustomed. The stocks and bonds do not have to be liquidated upon your death because the trust owns the assets, and the trust survives. When your spouse passes, the assets are divided pursuant to your wishes as set forth in the trust document. At that point in time, the trust can be dissolved.

The most common advantage of a revocable trust is that it avoids probate. A will, unlike a trust, must be probated. Probate is simply the process of administering your estate. Probate means that the court in your state is responsible for validating the will, certifying the executor, and monitoring the actions of your executor.[10] For example, your executor cannot take possession of your assets and start distributing them to your heirs until officially appointed by the court. If there is a dispute regarding the will, the court oversees the dispute. Whereas, in a revocable trust, the transfer of property to the hands of the successor trustee (the person who will oversee your trust when you die) happens automatically. This results in continuity without delay in the management of your assets. This is a common complaint against probate since the court process can move slowly and resulting in a delay in disposition of your assets to your beneficiaries. The other common complaint with the probate process centers on the cost of probate and specifically the potentially high fees charged by attorneys. Some attorneys charge a percentage of the estate to handle the probate process. The problem with this approach to fees is that it does not always bear a reasonable relationship to the work and responsibility involved.

Subject to the advice of your estate planning attorney and your accountant who is also the check on the estate attorney, it is essential to have a will as stated above but, as your assets grow, it may be beneficial to also establish a revocable trust that will hold most of your assets. Under this arrangement, the will becomes a spill over, or catch all for any minor assets that are not held in the revocable trust where most of your assets reside. As stated above, the advantage is that you avoid probate fees and there is a seamless transition of your assets from you to your trustee.

A final type of trust to be aware of is an *Irrevocable Trust*. This type or trust cannot be modified or terminated without the consent of the beneficiary or beneficiaries of the trust. The grantor (the one who gives the money) gives up all right of ownership in the assets placed in the trust. Irrevocable trusts are generally set up to minimize estate taxes and protect assets since anything contributed is outside your control and not owned by you. As a physician and a potential tar-

---

[10] To avoid confusion, in the above example, if you have a will, as long as your assets are jointly in you and your spouse's name, the mechanics are essentially the same as a trust with the executor taking the place of the co-trustee to administer the will. The only difference is that a will must be probated, and a trust continues with no delay regarding distribution of assets.

get for lawsuits, an irrevocable trust is a potential tool to shield you from lawsuits. Contrast this with a revocable trust which allows the grantor to modify the trust but loses certain benefits such as creditor protection.

How does an Irrevocable Trust work? As the grantor, you contribute assets to the trust, and they are held on behalf of the beneficiary. A trustee is appointed, and that trustee cannot be you or your spouse. The trustee must be independent but can be the beneficiary depending on the circumstances of the trust.

The most common use of an irrevocable trust is for estate planning purposes. Specifically, as discussed above, the current estate tax exemption is $11.7 million per individual or $23.4 million for couples. This means that the first $23.4 million of your estate is not subject to the estate tax upon your death and your spouse's death. However, anything in excess is taxed up to 40%. As discussed earlier, this exemption amount is likely to go down to approximately $6.2 million for each individual but this could change, and it is likely to go down and not up.

An example is illustrative. You and your spouse have three children and establish three irrevocable trusts contributing a total of $23.4 million divided equally to the trusts. The beneficiary are your three children. The trust document appoints your best friend as the co-trustee of each trust along with each child. No monies can be used from the trust unless both trustees (your child and your friend) agree. In addition, you and your spouse decide that your friend maintains his role as co-trustee until each child reaches the age of 30. Once they are 30 years old, they are free to be the sole trustee but may only use the monies in the trust with certain limitations that you and your spouse set forth in the trust document. This uses your one-time estate tax exemption of $23.4 million but gets the money out of your estate and limits the amount of estate tax you will pay, particularly if the exemption goes down as expected. It also establishes a legacy for your children but with limitations that you set. Another advantage is that the amount in each trust is not subject to community property if you child marries and gets divorced meaning that the ex-spouse cannot make a claim against the trust.[11] A final advantage is that an irrevocable trust keeps your estate from appreciating because you move the assets from your estate to the trust and there is no taxable event unless monies are taken out of the trust. This means that the assets can continue to appreciate without being subject to estate tax as long as they are not taken out of the trust. For example, your estate is worth $50 million dollars. If you allow it to continue to appreciate, any amount currently over $23.4 million will be subject to the estate tax upon your death and your spouse's death. However, if you use the exemption and move $23.4 million to an irrevocable trust, that $23.4 million can grow and its growth will not be subject to estate tax because it is held in the irrevocable trust. This trust continues in perpetuity unless the monies are pulled out by your children. In sum, irrevocable trusts are an important tool in many people's estate plan. They can be used to lock-in your estate tax exemption before it drops, keep appreciation on assets from inflating your taxable estate, and protect assets from creditors.[12] Finally, there is a cost to establish and maintain trusts so weighing the benefits is very important. Your accountant and lawyer should advise you on this, but they are wonderful tools to have in your personal finance arsenal and have specific uses.

---

[11] Connecticut may consider trust assets as community property.

[12] While beyond the discussion in this book, irrevocable trusts can be utilized to maintain eligibility for Medicaid benefits. This is especially applicable if there are dependents who are disabled or have long term disabilities.

CONCEPT 12:
Personal finance can be summarized as follows:

- Buy assets not liabilities. Assets are items that appreciate, and liabilities depreciate.
- Your goal is to be wealthy or balance sheet rich holding assets that appreciate and generate passive income. Earning a high income is good but it means nothing if you have no cattle.
- To become wealthy, commit to your Investment Plan: "Pay Yourself First" - put 10% to 20% of your take home pay in low cost, indexed mutual funds tracking major market indexes each month.
- Be a committed investor by automatically debiting your investment each month so you won't be tempted to forego your Investment Plan.
- Playing good defense is critical and this means controlling your expenses so you can follow your investment plan.
- Debt is the anchor to building wealth. Pay off your bad debt and only maintain debt that is used to augment your net worth.
- Developing an insurance strategy is very important. It is your key risk management tool.
- Understand that taxes are your biggest expense and understand how they work. Tax avoidance is illegal, tax deferment within the law is smart.
- Use estate planning tools to provide for your loved ones. Have a will, a living will (advanced directives) and a power of attorney.
- Use revocable trusts and irrevocable trusts to your advantage.

Chapter VIII
Investing and Retirement Planning

In the personal finance chapter, creating real wealth versus relative wealth was emphasized. Real wealth is defined as being balance sheet rich by acquiring assets that generate passive income and harness the great power of compound interest resulting in complete financial independence. The way to achieve this is by being a committed investor and Paying Yourself First. "The philosophy of the rich and the poor is this: the rich invest their money and spend what is left. The poor spend their money and invest what is left." – Robert Kiyosaki.

In order to really understand why this works, let's delve into these concepts further because it is essential to have a grounding in investment theory and why markets work the way they do so that you won't be tempted by charlatans and those promising tempting returns that almost never transpire.

As we continue to say, generating passive income is the key to real wealth (balance sheet rich). In his excellent books, Rich Dad Poor Dad and its sequel, Cash Flow Quadrant, Robert Kiyosaki discusses how to generate passive income:

He breaks down occupations into four distinct categories and assigns a letter to them. E is for employee, S is for the self-employed or small business owners and professionals such as physicians, B is a business owner, and I is an investor. Employees work for money, the self-employed work for themselves, a business owner works for the business and investors have people work for them.

He emphasizes that the business owner (a "B") has the ability to step away from the business for more than a year because he or she hires managers to run the operation. The business owner does not have to be there every day. Further, most of the wealth generated by a business is when it is sold, and that sale is subject to capital gains tax - currently approximately 50% of the ordinary income rate (regular wages). See Taxes. Similarly, investors (I) are paid dividends, taxed again at approximately 50% of the ordinary income rate and pay capital gains when the business is sold. Business owners and investors use the concept of leverage, or having others work for you, since they are not obligated daily to tend the business so that they can spend time generating income in other ways. They leverage by lawfully paying less taxes since long term dividend income and capital gains are taxed at an advantageous rate. This is why we emphasize the concept of being an investor so that you are creating passive income.

As a physician, you fall under the employee or self-employed category. There is nothing wrong with being a "S" or "E", as long as you are also an "I" by continually investing and harnessing the power and leverage of dividend and capital gain income so that eventually you generate enough passive income to cover your monthly expenses and achieve *real wealth* = financial independence. When you achieve real wealth, you are making money while playing golf or tennis because you are not required to work. This gives you options in life to continue to work for enjoyment, pursue your hobbies and passions and spend time with your family.

Chapter 8 - Investing and Retirement Planning

Investing Pitfalls

Now that you understand the goal is to achieve real wealth by generating passive income and that can only be accomplished by investing, it is time to understand how to invest.[13] You can be a committed investor and Pay Yourself First, and still not achieve material wealth if you make poor investment choices. There is no free lunch and risk and return are linked. Even seasoned investors make mistakes, so the key is to limit those mistakes. There are good investments and bad investments and understanding the pitfalls are essential to mitigating mistakes.

The most common mistakes are natural and seem logical, so you must have a solid grounding in theory so that you do not fall prey to them. We will explain the conclusions in detail further in this chapter, but the following is a list of those common mistakes and a brief explanation.

---

[13] I am not a professional investment advisor and do not purport to give you professional advice. Rather, I am a successful investor and the suggestions in this book are exactly the same that I give my children. There are no guarantees that markets will rise, and past returns are not a guarantee of future returns. The best we can do is to apply logic and understand that risk and return are intertwined so the reader must make his or her own decisions.

Chapter 8 - Investing and Retirement Planning

Mistake	Reality
You pull money out of the market when it goes down and invest back when it goes up.	Market timing has proven to be nearly impossible for investors because of the speed of information that is disseminated, and the time it takes for an average investor to make a trade is much slower than for an institutional investor. You are a physician, not a trader. Investors often underperform the broad market because they make investing decisions based on emotions. For example, investors may buy when a stock price is too high, only because others are buying it, or they may sell on one piece of bad news.
You watch CNBC and read the Wall Street Journal to gather tips to beat the market.	Markets are efficient. Information is almost instantaneously absorbed, and the price of stocks adjusts in seconds. CNBC exists to entertain, not help you beat the market since their experts have no insider knowledge, just opinions and hunches because if they had insider knowledge, they would be violating the law.
You use money managers who promise returns that beat the market and show you data that "proves" they beat the market.	The data is compelling. Professional money managers have not been able to beat a simple indexed mutual fund such as the S&P 500 over the long run particularly after considering their fees, the costs of trades and taxes. They may show you data for a specific time period, but over the long run (10, 15, 20 years) the results are very telling. Anyone can get lucky for a time, but they fight an uphill battle similar to a gambler. The house (the market) always wins in the long run.

Chapter 8 - Investing and Retirement Planning

Mistake	Reality
You believe that you are smarter than the average investor and can use your superior intellect to beat the market.	If professional money managers, can't do it, why do you believe that you can? Don't be seduced by short run wins, someone has to win a coin flipping contest.
Advisers, brokers, and other professionals promote their ability to ferret out the underperforming managers and find outliers who will outperform.	Research has consistently shown that professional investors have not been able to find outlier managers any better than individual investors. As one well-researched paper concluded: "We find no evidence that investment consultant recommendations add value."

Perhaps the hardest challenge is overcoming your emotions; when the market goes down and investors get nervous and stop their investment plan or worse sell holdings; or when it goes up precipitously, and investors believe that they can't lose and then take disproportioned risks. All that glitters is not gold, and bubbles and crashes or corrections happen with regularity in all markets. They are expected and regular so investors should not panic but continue playing the long game and not jump on the latest craze, but rather stay the course with your investment strategy. This is not based on faith, rather it is based on logic. We will explain why later in this chapter, but let's examine some famous bubbles to solidify your foundation in investment theory so you will not be tempted to deviate from your plan. History repeats itself and bubbles come and go. The following are some famous ones.

In the 17th century, Tulip Mania was the first documented *speculative bubble*[14], or situation in which asset prices rose much higher than the underlying fundamentals could be reasonably justified. It occurred in Holland in the 1630s when the tulip bulb was first introduced to Europe and became a fashionable item. Contract prices, or the right to purchase the bulbs, reached extraordinarily high levels mostly starting in 1634 and then dramatically collapsing in February 1637. The term "tulip mania" is now often used metaphorically to refer to any large economic bubble when asset prices deviate from intrinsic value, or the underlying fundamentals that can be justified for the asset. Essentially, the price of the tulip bulbs, that bloom only once a year, began to rise rapidly as demand increased. Then, the market crashed in 1637 when speculators felt that the prices peaked and began selling off the tulip bulb contracts causing a rush of others who followed in herdlike fashion.

Another great and more recent example is the dotcom or Internet bubble of the late 1990s. This was a stock market bubble caused by excessive speculation of internet related companies. In the 1990s, it was a period of massive growth in the use and adoption of the internet. Hence, money flowed into internet companies based on speculation that they would be profitable in the future and these companies would become the next Apple or Microsoft. However, most of the companies were startups, losing money and burning cash but it was replenished by investor demand for these stocks. Speculators were quoted as experts saying things like, "profits don't matter anymore" and "it's different this time." Unfortunately for them, accounting scandals, excessive losses, a Japanese recession and bankruptcies caused the bubble to burst when the cash infusion from private equity firms and the public markets dried up because investors could not stand long term losses and lack of profit. Between 1995 and its peak in March 2000, the Nasdaq stock market index rose 400%, only to fall 78% from its peak by October 2002, giving up all its gains during the bubble.

---

[14] The term "bubble" is metaphor indicating that the price of a stock or item is inflated and fragile – expanding based on nothing but air, and vulnerable to a sudden burst.

Other recent bubbles include the housing crisis of 2002 to 2006 memorialized in the excellent film and better book "The Big Short," the 1997 Asian financial crisis and the 1980 Silver Thursday collapse. The lesson from bubbles is that they occur with regularity, and you should not be surprised by them and stay away from their siren song. Indicators and warning signs of bubbles: "This time everything is different," the market draws an increasing number of speculators, rapidly rising prices, increased media coverage, low-interest rates facilitate speculation. Is the next bubble cryptocurrency? It certainly has the characteristics of one, but the jury is still out. Remember that bubbles occur in narrow or specific markets (tulip bulbs, real estate). Stay the course with your investment plan because the good news is that eventually true value is recognized and purchasing the broad market keeps you out of the narrow waters where bubbles occur.

CONCEPT 13: Think of the market like a sports car. You don't want to redline it all the time, the engine needs a break so it can perform and finish the race, so welcome market corrections and bubbles. They will occur with regularity so don't be surprised by them. The market corrects itself over the long run and true value is recognized. Avoid the siren song of bubbles and diversify your portfolio, stay the course, and stick with your investment plan.

Mutual Funds: Stock Picking Managers Versus Index Strategies

Before we start discussing investment theory let's define a couple of key terms.

A *mutual fund* is an investment fund that pools money from many investors and invests the money in securities such as stocks, bonds, and short-term debt. Investors buy shares in mutual funds. Each share represents an investor's part ownership in the fund and the income it generates. When we use the term "fund" in this book we are referring to a mutual fund.

A *passively managed index fund* (also referred to as an index fund) is a mutual fund whose investment securities are not chosen by a portfolio manager, but instead are automatically selected to match an index or part of the market. For example, an S&P 500 index fund is a passively managed fund that mimics the *S&P 500 index*, an index of the 500 largest companies in the United States.

An *actively managed fund* is the opposite of an index fund and has a manager or team making decisions on the underlying portfolio allocation, otherwise not adhering to a passive investment strategy. These funds are managed by professionals who strive to outperform the market. Many call these strategies actively managed funds, as they actively pick individual stocks or bonds that they suggest will add Alpha or outperformance on a risk adjusted basis.

The real difference may come down to one primary thing: Fees

A passively managed fund charges on average 0.09%[15] of your investment to manage the mutual fund whereas, an actively managed mutual fund must pay the professionals for their time, research and expertise selecting stocks. The average fee for an active fund is 0.82% as you will see below but may be actually higher due to transaction costs and taxes. The fee for an active managed fund is estimated to

---

[15] Many mutual funds especially the Schwab and Vanguard funds charge management fees much lower than 0.09%. For example, the Schwab S&P 500 Index Fund has an expense ratio of 0.02%.

be closer to 1.20%. As covered in detail below, note that the 1.11% difference between an actively managed fund (1.20%) and the average passively managed fund (0.09%) makes a huge difference in returns over time and will greatly impact how much money you will retain from your investments.

How Markets Work

As we continue the building blocks of understanding investment theory, we will examine its core tenets to explain the logic of investing.

1. Efficient Markets

Eugene Fama, the Nobel Prize winning economist, defined a market to be "informationally efficient" - prices at each moment <u>incorporate all available information</u> about future values. This is known as *Efficient Market Theory*. Informational efficiency is a natural consequence of competition, relatively free entry, and the speed and low cost of information. If there is a signal, not incorporated in market prices, that future values will be high, competitive traders will buy on that signal. In doing so, they bid the price up, until it fully reflects the information in the signal. The main prediction of efficient markets is exactly that <u>stock price movements are unpredictable</u> because if all the information at any given moment is disseminated, any new information is by its nature unpredictable because no one can predict what will actually happen in the future. Those who forecast the future are offset by those who forecast the opposite and the stock price reaches its equilibrium point.

Sports betting is not that different than traditional investing and provides a great example. In fact, the NFL is the model of an efficient market because there are so many people studying and analyzing the NFL that the point spreads reach a stasis or level almost as soon as they come out since so much information is out there and half the people feel the spread is too high and the other half feel the spread is too low, so it settles in quickly. Let's say that Tampa is favored by 6 points over the Cowboys. It may move based on predictions and the whims of the betters more toward Tampa or the Cowboys but not materially. Now however, let's say that Tom Brady breaks his hand in practice and is out for the game. The line will move immediately and may move to now favor the Cowboys. The point is that Tom Brady breaking his hand is unpredictable and the line only moves when this information comes out.

The Bottom Line: Markets are Efficient[16]

2. Randomly Walking

Similarly, if markets are informationally efficient, fundamental analysis performed by investment firms has no power to select stocks, and professional active managers should do no better at picking stock portfolios than monkeys with darts.[17] See Appendix I. This is a remarkable proposition. In any other field of human endeavor, seasoned professionals systematically outperform amateurs. But other fields are not so ruthlessly competitive as financial markets. The data backs this up. According to S&P SPIVA, a research arm of Standard and Poor's, of all domestic actively managed equity funds, 88.4% underperformed their respective benchmark over the last 15 years. The ones that did outperform will likely not do it going forward. As research has shown, "No large-cap, mid-cap, or small-cap

---

[16] Are markets completely efficient? Probably not since there may be markets that are not followed closely and the prices may not incorporate all available information, but for purposes of this book, we are discussing major markets such as the U.S. stock and bond market, the largest and hence most efficient markets. The efficient market theory has its critics (and most of them are investment professionals who make a comfortable living giving financial advice), and the reader should take those into account but the evidence that professionals cannot outperform the market in the long run is compelling and hence, bolstering the argument that markets are efficient.

[17] *"A blindfolded monkey throwing darts at a newspaper's financial pages could select a portfolio that would do just as well as one carefully selected by experts."* Burton Malkiel, author of A Random Walk Down Wall Street. There have been several monkey throwing contests conducted over the years that have included monkeys, cats and blindfolded interns throwing darts at a board. The results are inconclusive with the experts winning some and the "monkeys" winning some; however, if there is really expertise shouldn't the experts win all of these? In fact, Warren Buffet the famous investor bet $1 million of his own money that the Vanguard S&P 500 Index fund could beat hedge fund managers. Buffett's ultimately successful contention was that, including fees, costs and expenses, a S&P 500 index fund would outperform a hand-picked portfolio of hedge funds over 10 years. The bet pit two basic investing philosophies against each other index and active investing. Warren Buffet won – it was not close.

funds managed to remain in the top quartile at the end of [a forward looking] five-year measurement period."[18] Stocks revert to the mean. Put another way, someone has to win a coin flipping contest but it is unlikely the same person will win it a second time. There are no professional coin flipping champions.

> CONCEPT 14: Professionally managed portfolios over the long run have not beaten their benchmarked indexes over the course of several studies. In addition, after factoring in cost, the data strongly correlates with efficient market theory – markets are efficient and hence professionals have no more of an advantage than amateurs (or monkeys).

---

[18] https://fwpwealth.com/say-it-aint-so-joe-again/

3. Diversification and Modern Portfolio Theory

If markets are efficient, as is proposed, and the experts cannot reliably predict movement, how do you construct a reasonable investment portfolio? *Modern portfolio* theory espoused by Harry Markowitz at the University of Chicago where he won a Nobel Prize in economics, attempts to answer the question of portfolio construction. His assertion is that <u>risk and return are inextricably linked but through *diversification* one can lower the portfolio's risk</u> for a given return expectation (alternately, no additional expected return can be gained without increasing the risk of the portfolio).

He goes on to assert that stocks face both systematic risk—market risks such as interest rates and recessions—as well as unsystematic risk—issues that are specific to each stock, such as management changes or poor sales. Proper diversification of a portfolio can't prevent systematic risk, but it can dampen, if not eliminate, unsystematic risk.

A diversified portfolio is a collection of different investments that combine to reduce an investor's overall risk profile. Diversification includes owning stocks from several different industries, countries, and risk profiles, as well as other investments such as bonds commodities, and real estate. These various assets work together to <u>reduce</u> an investor's risk of a permanent loss of capital and their portfolio's overall <u>volatility</u>. In exchange, the returns from a diversified portfolio tend to be lower than what an investor might earn *if* they were able to pick a single winning stock.

> CONCEPT 15: Diversify - Don't put all your eggs in one basket.

4. Time and the Magic of Compounding

At this point, we know that markets are mostly efficient, professional money managers cannot beat the market in the long run particularly after factoring in their costs, and you must have a diversified portfolio in order to reduce your risk. The last leg of the investment theory stool is time and how time and compound interest work in your favor. With these tools, we can then begin to get into the specifics of portfolio construction.

This brings us back full circle to our discussion in Chapter 7 about the power of compound interest. Compounding - the money you invest and save earns interest, and then you earn interest on the money you originally save, plus on the interest you've accumulated. As your savings grow, you earn interest on a bigger and bigger pool of money.[19]

The Key to Wealth

The example below is empirical evidence to prove why you must Pay Yourself First and be a committed investor every month. Harnessing the power of compound interest through systematically investing is the Key to Wealth.

Example: Let's say Savannah, age 20, invests $1,000 today at a very reasonable 7.2% growth rate.

- If she doesn't touch it until age 70, her money will increase by 32x, or around $32,000.

- But what if Savannah waited another 10 years, until she was 30 years old, to invest that $1,000 and leave it be until retirement? Sarah would have just $16,000 or about half.

---

[19] To clarify, for stocks or stocks held in a mutual fund, the fund pays dividends in lieu of interest and then those dividends are reinvested perpetuating the compounding, so you are paid dividends on a greater amount the next period because you reinvested the dividends.

- If she waits until age 40, she'd be left with half again, or $8,000.

- The real kicker or "where it gets really magical," is that if Savannah were to invest that $1,000 at age 20 and contribute $83 a month (around $1,000 a year) until retirement, then by age 70, she'd have **$465,000.**

CONCEPT 16: Time & Compounded Interest are your Friend – be a Committed Investor

5. Costs and Why they Matter

Time, Risk and Return are the links of portfolio construction, but Costs are the weight. The investment industry rarely if ever shows _net_ returns - the returns after costs. John Bogle, the founder of Vanguard calls this the Tyranny of Compounding: a higher cost investment loses ever more ground to a lower cost one over time. For example, a $10,000 investment growing at **12%** over 40 years is $931,000. However, the same investment growing at **10%** (2% annual equity fund expenses, taxes, and fees) grows to only $453,00, or less than 50%!

The average active managed mutual fund cost is 0.82%, the average passive managed index fund cost is 0.09% or 1/9th and many passively managed index funds have much lower fees. However, for the average active managed mutual fund this doesn't factor in transaction fees, advisor fees and taxes.[20] Why? The active mutual manager charges a management fee of 0.82% for their "expertise" and as part of this, then they make trades to attempt to beat the market and those trades generate transaction fees and taxes when a security is sold for a profit. This makes the real fee closer to 1.20% but it is suspected that the cost is higher. However, for comparison purposes, we will be conservative and give the active manager the benefit of the doubt and use 1.20% as the effective management fee in the following example.

Example: $10,000 earning an 8.0% average annual return over 20 years

Active Managed Fund		Index Fund	
Management Fee	0.82%	Management Fee	0.04%[21]
Transaction and Other Costs	0.38%	Transaction and Other Costs	0.05%
Final Amount	$38,813	Final Amount	$48,395

The difference is ($9,582).

---

[20] Source: Asset-weighted averages from 2016 data from the Investment Company Institute.

[21] For this example, we use Vanguard Total Stock Market with a minimum $10,000 balance. Passive funds generate some transaction fees, and this is reflected in the example, but they are much less than active funds because they are purchasing and not actively trading (buying and selling constantly).

Chapter 8 - Investing and Retirement Planning

But this gets worse. What if you hire a money[22] manager to manage your money and they charge you 1.0% of your assets under management every year to provide this service? You will be left with only $31,810.

Final Returns to Investor of $10,000 earning an 8.0% average annual return over 20 years.

Index Fund	$48,395
Actively Managed Mutual Fund	$38,813
Actively Managed Mutual Fund + Fee based Money Manager	$31,810

Bottom Line: The actively managed fund and the money manager eat up 34% of your return! Is it reasonable to believe that they can overcome this handicap through their expertise with the strong evidence that the market is efficient and nearly 90% all domestic actively managed equity funds underperforming their benchmarks?

The chart below is yet another example of costs and how they impact the investor.

Index Fund versus Managed Fund
Average Profit on Initial Investment of $10,000, 1980-2005

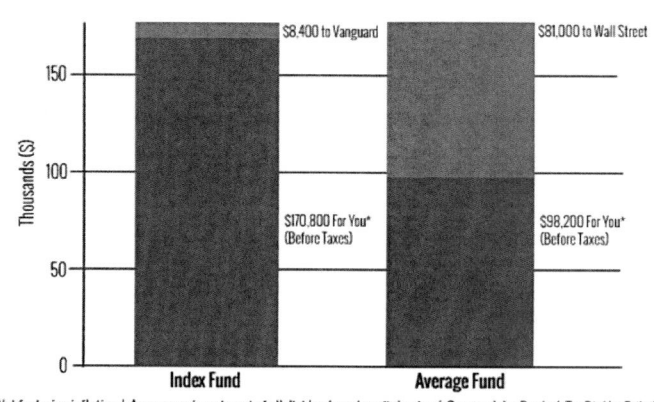

- Index Fund: $8,400 to Vanguard | $170,800 For You* (Before Taxes)
- Average Fund: $81,000 to Wall Street | $98,200 For You* (Before Taxes)

*Not factoring inflation | Assumes reinvestment of all dividends and capital gains | Source: John Bogle | TooBigHasFailed.org

---

[22] As a point of clarification, it is important to distinguish a money manager who advises you on your portfolio and which funds or stocks to pick from the actively managed mutual fund manager who charges a fee (0.82% in our example). Money managers typically charge a percentage of your portfolio to provide advisory services. The fees range from 0.50% to up to 2.00%. Finally, there is the wealth manager who provides consulting services related to your total financial plan and works on an hourly basis. We recommend the wealth manager as an important part of your Tribe.

Costs and Why They Matter Part II

In 1986, three economists (Brinson/Hood/Beebower) published an article using data from 91 large U.S. Pension plans over the 1974-1983 period that indicated that <u>investment policy rather than investment strategy</u> accounts for 93.6% of the return of these funds. They followed up with another study in 1991 showing the same results.

What does this mean? It means that about 94% of your returns are based on your asset allocation (stock to bond mix such as 70% stock and 30% bonds) and not on which stocks or bonds you pick, diminishing the role of an active money manager since investment strategy is diminished. Additionally, costs account for the other 6% of your returns. Put another way, if stock picking strategy has marginal impact on returns, the lower an investor pays for management, the higher the expected return. In sum, the cost of investing goes hand in hand with asset allocation as the key determinant of long-term returns.

Bottom Line: If asset allocation, rather than which securities you pick is the main determinant of returns, then professional managers on average should not add value. Once fees including management fees, transactional fees and taxes are factored, this difference becomes more acute.

Investment Theory Summary

Before we delve into portfolio construction, it is important that you understand the fundamentals of investment theory and why this is correct to prevent you from diverging from your course when the next "big thing" comes along, or you are being pitched the benefits of a money manager. Countless physicians have been taken advantage of because they did not understand this, believed money management was too complex or believed they knew better. There is an entire industry built on managing money because it is very profitable for the money managers. There is too much evidence to show that the money managers who advise you on your portfolio and the actively managed mutual fund managers are unable to add value and beat a simple index mutual fund strategy over the long term and this is compounded by the fees they charge, and other costs associated with actively managing financial portfolios. They are simply playing at a disadvantage. Anyone can show that they have beaten the market in the short run, but over time, the house catches up to them. So, in summary it is proposed that:

1. *Markets are Efficient in the long run and thus, stock picking is likely a loser's game – there are no professional roulette players because the house edge (fees and costs) catches up to them in the long run.*

2. *Diversify - Don't put all your eggs in one basket. You want to own a diversified portfolio of stocks and bonds. This is how you manage risk.*

3. *Time & Compounded Interest are your Friend – be a committed investor so Pay Yourself First.*

4. *Risk, Return and Costs are forever linked (the Eternal Triangle) – Since the majority of your returns are based on your stock to bond mix and not necessarily which stocks or bonds you pick as long as you have a diversified portfolio, costs are the anchor and impact returns severely. Limit your cost and achieve high returns.*

5. *Stay the Course - Develop a sound investment allocation that fits your risk tolerance and don't be seduced by the siren song of promised returns. Rely on the data grounded in sound theory and remember that true value is eventually recognized.*

Risk and Return Revisited

Portfolios are made up of different investment instruments, such as stocks and bonds. Each has a return that's based on the level of risk an investor is willing to take. See Modern Portfolio Theory above. Investors can make comparisons using historical data to determine the total real returns from different combinations of assets over short or long-term periods but must understand that past returns are not guarantee of future returns.

Over a long period of time, the average return for stocks is higher than other investment instruments. Why? Stocks are riskier than bonds such as a U.S. Treasury note and must compensate the investor for the additional risk. A *bond* is a debt obligation of the issuer. There are government bonds such as treasuries issued by the United States government, corporate bonds issued by corporations and municipal bonds issued by municipalities. In the event that the entity that issues the bond goes bankrupt, the debt or bond holders get their money back -before the investors or stockholders - and thus bonds are less riskier than stocks. Remember that risk and return are inextricably linked. The higher the risk, the higher the required return to investors or they will move to safer investments. A U.S. treasury note is considered nearly riskless and thus the return, or interest it pays, is lower. Conversely, a *stock* is a share in a company and some companies do well and some do not. Thus, stocks must offer a higher return than treasury bonds. This is why we state that in the long run, true value is recognized.

This concept was postulated in 1759 and later more famously in 1776 by a Scottish economist by the name of Adam Smith who described the *hidden hand* that impacts markets. The hidden hand is a metaphor that suggest that the market will find equilibrium without interventions forcing it into unnatural patterns. When supply and demand find equilibrium naturally, oversupply and shortages are avoided. To put in a more practical sense, let's say you live on a remote island and there is one bicycle maker, he can charge whatever price that he wants since he has a captured market. However, a competitor enters the market. This requires the original maker to stay competitive by dropping his price and increasing quality to keep up. Others enter the market until the price and quality reach a level that allow the manufacturers to stay in business and make a reasonable profit.

What does this mean? Over time, stocks must return more than corporate bonds which, in turn must return more than U.S. treasuries because risk and return must eventually be recognized. Adam Smith's hidden hand works to find equilibrium between risk and returns. This is a fundamentally important concept that will help you when others are panicking or showing irrational exuberance. Stay the course with your plan - the market will work itself out.

> CONCEPT 17: Water finds its own level – over a period of time, stocks will offer higher returns than bonds because risk and return are linked. If stocks do not return more than bonds, investors will move money to safer investments (bonds) and the cash outflow will, in turn, lower the price of stocks, which will then make them cheap enough to offer the type of return that will bring back investors. Thus, the market finds its own level balancing risk and return with higher expected returns favoring the riskier investments.

Chapter IX
Portfolio Construction

This book emphasized the concept of Pay Yourself First – put 10% to 20% or more of your taxable net income (income after taxes) in low cost, indexed mutual funds and bond funds. Importantly, harnessing the snowball effect or power of compound interest, following a regular automatic saving plan, and not deviating from that investment plan is integral. This transitioned into understanding the 'why' of this because not blindly following advice is one of the other core concepts of this book. It is submitted that major markets are efficient and thus paying someone to manage your portfolio is probably a loser's game because managers cannot overcome the cost drag those managers charge.[23] Holding a large number of equities (stocks) and bonds provides diversification and lowers your risk and the best way to do this is through mutual funds or exchange traded funds that provide diversification. Furthermore, as explained above, the stock to bond mix that you hold based on your risk tolerance has more to do with your return than actually which stocks and bonds that you pick assuming you have a diverse portfolio. However, the anchor is costs. Costs drag down your portfolio and must be managed in

---

[23] We distinguish this from paying a wealth manager to assist you with your entire financial situation on a fee basis. See Building Your External Tribe and footnote 22.

order to maximize returns. The good news is that this can be easily achieved, and just as Occam's Razor[24] postulated, sometimes the simplest answer is the best one, so let's begin constructing a solid portfolio by following the recommend steps.

Portfolio Construction

Step 1: Determine your Risk Tolerance

The following are historical returns of sample portfolios courtesy of Vanguard.[25]

HISTORICAL INDEX RISK/RETURN (1926–2019)

Portfolio Average	Annual Return
0% Equity, 100% Bond	5.3%
30% Equity, 70% Bond	7.21%
50% Equity, 50% Bond	8.29%
60% Equity, 40% Bond	8.77%
80% Equity, 20% Bond	9.61%
100% Equity, 0% Bond	10.29%

---

[24] Occam's Razor - the simplest explanation is usually the best one. The idea is always to cut out extra unnecessary bits, hence the name "razor."

[25] From Vanguard: "Past performance is no guarantee of future returns. The performance of an index is not an exact representation of any particular investment, as you cannot invest directly in an index. When determining which index to use and for what period, we selected the index that we deemed to be a fair representation of the characteristics of the referenced market, given the information currently available. For U.S. stock market returns, we used the Standard & Poor's 90 Index from 1926 through March 3, 1957; the S&P 500 Index from March 4, 1957, through 1974; the Dow Jones Wilshire 5000 Index from 1975 through April 22, 2005; the MSCI US Broad Market Index from April 23, 2005, through June 2, 2013; and the CRSP US Total Market Index thereafter. For U.S. bond market returns, we used the S&P High Grade Corporate Index from 1926 through 1968, the Citigroup High Grade Index from 1969 through 1972, the Lehman Brothers U.S. Long Credit AA Index from 1973 through 1975, the Bloomberg Barclays U.S. Aggregate Bond Index from 1976 through 2009, and the Bloomberg Barclays U.S. Aggregate Float Adjusted Index thereafter."

Remember, that you must have the patience to allow the markets to work and water to find its level. For example, despite the fact that the 100% stock portfolio returns much more, if you held 100% equities (stocks) for that period, during your worst year, your investments would have plummeted 41%. If you had a 50/50 portfolio your worst year would have only shown a loss of 23%. However, risk and return are forever intertwined, but patience pays off and recall the *Tyranny of Compounding* example: a $10,000 investment growing at 12% over 40 years is $931,000 as compared to one at 10% that grows to only $453,00, or less than 50%. The advice is to control your emotions, stick with your plan (stay the course), turn off CNBC, and let the markets work over the long run because value must be recognized, and stocks and bonds must generate a reasonable return or investors will find other places to put their money. Your understanding of the whys of investment theory are your rock to keep you from making irrational decisions.

Step 2: Utilize Retirement Accounts.

Use the tax system to accelerate growth of your portfolio. An IRA or Individual Retirement Account allows investors to contribute up to $6,000 ($7,000 if 50 or older) per year and permits the monies to grow tax deferred until they are pulled out at retirement when presumably you are in a lower tax bracket; however, regular IRAs have income limitations and if you are married and you make more than $125,000 the contribution is not tax deductible. Similar to an IRA is a Roth IRA. The Roth IRA is not tax deductible, but you do not pay any taxes upon retirement on any gains. Again, there are income limitations, and many physicians will phase out of the Roth IRA benefits.

The good news is that employers offer 401(k) plans if they are for-profit and 403(b) plans if a not-for-profit. There are several types of 401(k) and 403(b) plans but essentially, they are employer sponsored plans that give the employer the option to match the employee contribution. This is free money to you if your employer matches so maximize your contribution. If you are in private practice, you will also have a retirement plan that may be a 401(k) or a SEP-IRA. All of these plans allow you to contribute monies tax deductible and pay taxes on the gains at retirement, so they essentially grow tax free. There are also Roth style 401(k) plans that do not allow you to deduct your contributions, but the growth is tax free at retirement. This is where your wealth manager can really assist and guide you since they have specific rules and exclusions.

In summary, contributions from retirement plans are typically taken out of your paycheck or income from your practice and invested directly. It is suggested that you first contribute to any tax deferred plan and maximize the contribution to allow the growth to be deferred since many times the contribution is tax deductible and you will not be taxed on the dividends from the investments.[26]

Step 3: The Power of Simplicity

Once you contribute to your retirement plan, set up an account with a company who offers low-cost funds such as Vanguard, Schwab, or Fidelity. You can determine your asset allocation mix (stock to bond) and the account can be set up to auto debit out of your bank account. Use low cost, passively managed index funds that follow the S&P 500 or Wilshire 5000 for stocks, and indexes that follow the total bond market to construct a portfolio. For example, you decide on a 70% stock and 30% bond allocation and choose Vanguard Total Stock Market that indexes to the Wilshire 5000 index with a 0.14% management fee and is lowered to 0.04% once $10,000 is invested for your stock portion. Each month you have Vanguard debit 70% of your monthly contribution to invest in the fund. For the bond portion, you choose Schwab US Aggregate Bond Index with an expense ratio of 0.04% and have Schwab debit 30% of your monthly contribution amount to that fund.

---

[26] As clarification, when it is recommended to Pay Yourself First and contribute 10% to 20% of your "take home pay" we actually do count your retirement plan contributions that are taken out of your paycheck toward your investment plan.

Chapter 9 - Portfolio Construction

Alternatively, consider a *Target Date Retirement Fund* offered by Vanguard, Schwab, or Fidelity among others. This is a simple one-stop way to invest. Target-date funds are designed to age with you by automatically rebalancing your portfolio from growth investments toward more conservative ones as retirement nears. The reason for this is to mitigate the swings in your portfolio as you near retirement because as shown above, stocks can be volatile, so the target fund tampers the swings by shifting you more toward bonds as you age because they are less volatile.

As stated, a target fund automatically rebalances your portfolio with a mix of stocks, bonds, and money market accounts as you age. A target-date fund operates under an asset allocation formula that assumes you will retire in a certain year and adjusts its asset allocation model as it gets closer to that year. The target year is identified in the name of the fund. So, for instance, if you plan to retire in or near 2065, you pick a fund with 2065 in its name. With target date funds, you generally have three groups from which to choose. Each group is based on your risk tolerance, whether you are a conservative, aggressive, or moderate risk-taker. If you decide later that your risk tolerance has or needs to change as you get closer to retirement, you have the option of switching to a different risk level.

If you use a target date retirement fund, it is suggested that the fund use passively managed indexed funds for the reasons described in detail in this book. Additionally, the management fee for the fund should be no greater than 0.15%. For example, Schwab Target Date 2055 charges 0.08% management fee. Vanguard Target Retirement 2055 charges 0.15%. However, be aware that they may not be tax efficient since they are required to sell securities to rebalance over time and that triggers capital gain taxes. Certainly, they are very good choices for retirement accounts that are tax deferred. Also, some models suggest they are too conservative when the investor reaches age 50 - the fund holds too much in bonds and not enough in equities but this is risk tolerance dependent. Finally, target funds are slightly more costly than a simple two fund approach (e.g. S&P 500 or Wilshire 5000 fund and a total bond market fund) and as we know, costs matter. Overall, these are good choices and provide a simple, cost-effective approach to portfolio construction as long as you are aware of their drawbacks.

Another alternative is to use *ETFs or Exchange Traded Funds* to construct your portfolio. Again, these are offered by Schwab, Vanguard, Fidelity, and other investment firms. They are a basket of securities that track an underlying index and are traded on the major exchanges like the New York Stock Exchange and the NASDAQ. ETFs hold securities such as stocks and bonds and are traded daily. The site www.Investopedia.com suggests that the ETF structure results in more tax efficiency, too. Investors in ETFs and mutual funds are taxed each year based on the gains and losses incurred within the portfolios. But ETFs engage in less internal trading, and less trading creates fewer taxable events (the creation and redemption mechanism of an ETF reduces the need for selling). So, unless you invest through a 401(k) or other tax-favored vehicles, your mutual funds will distribute taxable gains to you, even if you simply hold the shares. Meanwhile, with an all-ETF portfolio, the tax will generally be an issue only if and when you sell the shares. ETFs are a solid alternative to mutual funds and your investment can be auto debited each month through your financial institution.

In summary, first and foremost regularly invest every month – Pay Yourself First. Next, the data shows that asset allocation or the stock to bond mix of your portfolio has the greatest impact on returns. Limiting your costs closely follows and is extraordinarily important since most funds and ETFs revert to the mean over the long run. Tax efficiency is important but is generally of lesser importance if you use index funds or indexed ETFs that are inherently tax efficient. A low-cost portfolio comprised of indexed stock funds that track the Wilshire 5000 or S&P 500 and a bond fund that tracks the bond market is perhaps the most effective choice. Target retirement funds are a good choice but be aware of their drawbacks as well as those of balanced funds. he formula for financial independence is shockingly simple: Invest 10% to 20% of your income each month using low cost, index funds or ETFs, and let the markets work themselves out. This is the advice I give my children and the advice I give to you.

Step 4: Buy and Hold

Once you have built your portfolio, buy, and hold to maximize your return regardless of fluctuations in the market. Never sell unless it is an emergency and please do not try to time the market. *Market Timing* is a controversial topic in the investment world whereby the investor makes decisions based on trends and pulls money out and then puts in back in when conditions are favorable. It is strongly recommended that you never do this because: 1) markets are generally efficient and stock prices adjust nearly instantaneously once information comes out; 2) buying and selling causes tax events (capital gains and ordinary income) See Taxes; 3) the upside to being right is not as great as the downside if you are wrong – you are not a speculator, you are an investor; and finally, 4) you are a physician and should focus on your practice. If you want to gamble, take a couple thousand to Las Vegas. That likely won't hurt you, gambling with your savings will. In summary, (and yes, it sounds like a broken record): Stay the course with your investment plan, get rich slowly and steadily. Par golf wins the Open.

However, this is not to say that you avoid looking at your portfolio regularly. In fact, on an quarterly basis, review your portfolio with your wealth manager and see if it has drifted away from the allocation that you desire.[27] This is called *Portfolio Drift*. For example, you choose a 70/30 stock to bond mix. Over the course of the year, the stock market outperforms the bond market, and you end up at 74/26. If you choose to rebalance, rather than sell stocks you can change your monthly allocation to get back in the 70/30 range and then reevaluate at the end of the year.

Some might say this is approach is too simple and is passive. How about if it was framed differently: Would you feel comfortable investing in a manner that has consistently outperformed the vast majority of top university endowments (organizations that have large investment teams and can access almost any manager they want to invest in)? Most would say, "yes, sign me up." Well…what was just described was a mix of index funds rebalanced only once a year.

---

[26] If you choose a target retirement fund, the allocation is done for you and rebalancing is not required but it does not negate the need to meet with your wealth manager at least yearly to look at your entire financial situation (investments, debt, insurance, estate plan).

Final Thoughts on Investing - The 9 Tenets of Financial Wisdom.

In his wonderful book Common Sense on Investing, John Bogle listed his 10 Pillars of Financial Wisdom. Borrowing from his list with some of my insights, the following are the lessons that I learned from him and submit to you for your consideration.

1. Occam's Razor/Simplicity is Key - investing is not as complicated as it looks. In fact, you can purchase low cost index funds, ETFs representing the broad market or a target retirement fund and sit on the beach and drink margaritas because the data is compelling - you will beat nearly all the professionals over time.

2. Pay Yourself First - Save at least 10% to 20% of your after-tax income and be a committed investor every month. Harnessing the power of compound interest through systematically investing in sound investments is the Key to Wealth.

3. The Beauty of *Diversity* – the power of index funds. Owning a combination of stocks and bonds combine to reduce an investor's overall risk profile.

4. Compound Interest and the Rule of 72 - *Time* is your friend, be a *compulsive investor* and allow the markets to work. Water finds its own level and true value will be recognized.

5. The Eternal Triangle: Risk, Return and Cost are intertwined.

6. Magnetism of the Mean - funds revert over time close to the averages or benchmarks. Professionals have yet to prove that they can beat the market over the long term, so asset allocation and costs have more to do with performance than tactical stock picking.

7. Costs Matter - Par golf wins the Open so stick with low-cost index funds and don't try to beat the market, buy funds that index to the market. They give you your best chance for success because they have the lowest cost and that puts them at a huge advantage.

8. Stay the Course and Don't Listen to the Siren Song of Professionals - the goal is to generate passive income through a committed investment plan so you can achieve financial independence. To quote financial author, Fred Schwed, "One can't say that figures lie. But figures as used in financial arguments, seem to have the bad habit of expressing a small part of the truth forcibly, and neglecting the other part, as do some people we know."

9. Buy and Hold (or why turning off the TV and sitting on the beach may be the best financial decision you ever make) – Market timing doesn't work. After you Pay Yourself First, unless it is an absolute emergency, hold your assets, never sell, let them compound, have a rebalancing plan and enjoy your margarita.

One last, definitive, and final word on index investing. Billionaire investor Warren Buffett has said that an S&P 500 index fund is the best investment most Americans can make. In fact, he stated that he wants his wife's money invested in such a fund after he's gone. This might seem a bit surprising since Buffett is well-known for his stock-picking ability.

Chapter X
The Role of Alternative Investments & Evaluating Ancillary Deals

Your portfolio does not have to consist of solely stocks and bonds. Remember your greatest asset is your income producing practice that begets investments and creates wealth and passive income. However, there are other investments, and they have a role but should make up only a small portion of your portfolio. We recommend no more than 10% of your net worth due to the fact that privately held investments carry more risk because of lack of liquidity (they are not traded on the exchanges so cannot be sold quickly) and lack of diversification (the investment is not comprised of 500 major corporations, rather it is a stand-alone venture). Thus, as you now know, with risk there must be higher returns for the investment to make sense. If a simple index fund like one following the S&P 500 has returned nearly 10% historically, your alternative investments must return higher to compensate for the risk. Remember, risk, return and cost are inextricably linked, so the return must be measured after fees to compensate you for the risk.

Chapter 10 - The Role of Alternative Investments & Evaluating Ancillary Deals

The following lists some common and not so common ventures that you will be approached to invest.

- Real Estate – Commercial real estate is perhaps a medical office building or apartments or an investment in rental properties. There are also REITs (real estate investment trusts) that trade on the stock exchanges that own a portfolio of properties.

- Precious Metals – Gold, Platinum and Silver. This is seen as a hedge against inflation. Precious metals have not provided good returns recently due to low inflationary pressure, but this may change in the future. In lieu of purchasing coins, there are precious metal ETFs and mutual funds.

- Commodities – Oil wells, Natural Gas and similar type of investments. They can be very lucrative ventures but are very dependent on the operator.

- Medical Ventures – This includes Surgery Centers, MRIs, Lithotripsy units etc. They can be very lucrative if operated properly but there are regulatory issues that must be reviewed before an investment is considered as well as partnership considerations listed below.

- Cryptocurrency – This is the hot topic at the time this book is being written. There are crypto ETFs that follow the market. The crypto market is very volatile and any move by governments to regulate will increase the volatility.

- Goldmines – If you are reading this book, there is little concern that you will invest in a goldmine.

- Car Washes, Restaurants and Nightclubs – If you do not know this business, avoid this business. There are countless stories of investors losing money in these ventures so be careful.

- Hamster Balls - This is included because it is my favorite of the investment schemes promoted to high-net-worth individuals. In fact, it was promoted to professional athletes and featured in an ESPN documentary entitled *Broke*. The promoter's concept was to sell blow up oversized plastic balls to people living in flood zones who can then put their belongings in them and then use a vacuum to blow them up so they will float away and be recovered in the future. It should come as no surprise that this venture was not successful, but it highlights a theme common to investment schemes in that the concept seems just plausible enough and the promised returns are very high.

A special note on Hedge Funds: The term "hedge fund" is really just a catch-all phrase. When you hear the term, remember that it does not mean lower risk or higher return. A hedge fund can invest in most anything they wish to invest in. They can be high, moderate, or low risk, and may or may not track the overall market. Importantly, remember the comments that we made earlier about fees and taxes, and how keeping both low may be the most important detriment of growing wealth? Hedge funds typically charge 2% per year plus 20% of profits. In total, independent researchers have estimated that this translates into total fees of between 4-6% per year, with investments wrapped up in an opaque, high turnover strategy that produces gains that are taxed at the highest ordinary income rates. As my friend Preston McSwain and seasoned investment adviser wrote for a peer reviewed trustee publication, "For me, what keeps me up at night is overly compensating my portfolio manager friends (performance fees), Wall Street Managing Directors (trading fees) and government coffers (high taxes). A sobering stream of logic goes as follows: if 5% of the 8,000 hedge fund managers can actually deliver on the required returns to overcome fees and taxes over the long-term, then why do the other 7,600 hedge fund managers exist?" One final caveat: It is important to keep in mind that, unfortunately, the rules around transparent disclosures are different concerning how private investments and hedge funds are marketed. Also, the calculation of performance and risk metrics can be quite different. Regulators are looking more into this and are issuing new investor risk alerts that include language like the following: "... misleading disclosures regarding performance and marketing… use of potentially misleading hedge clauses." Until potential changes materialize, treat this a warning to the investor. Preston McSwain wrote for the CFA Institute, "Unless you are well versed in the myriad ways private investment returns, standard deviation, and correlation metrics are calculated, and you are fully prepared to ask a lot of technical and often hard 'why' questions, buyer beware: "You may be purchasing so-called net returns that, 'over some periods of time,' 'no client received.'"

Related to this, keep in mind that many so-called alternative investments are often just alternative ways of packaging high fee and high tax strategies.

How to Evaluate Ancillary Ventures

First and foremost, a word of caution. While ancillary ventures have a place in your portfolio and most promoters are ethical, many of these ancillary ventures are disguised attempts to extract money from the investors through promoter fees, management fees, and related party transactions. The investor has little or no recourse because they signed a partnership agreement and subscription agreement allowing the promoter to have sole discretion operating the business. The cost of litigation far outweighs the damage to the investor resulting in an inevitable lesson learned. The good news is that much of this risk can be mitigated by using your Tribe.

First and foremost, as your first line of defense, your accountant, lawyer and business advisor should review these ventures carefully. Typically, you will receive a private placement memorandum that describes the venture, subscription agreement, and operating agreement or partnership agreement that you must review and sign before you invest. These documents are voluminous, and many (most) do not read them. You must have your Tribe members read them and you must do your best to understand them.

You must also perform due diligence with the assistance of your attorney, accountant and busines advisor. Questions to ask include:

- Evaluate the Promoter/Operator I: Experience – what experience do they have operating these types of ventures? How long have they been in business? What is their track record in other similar ventures, and can you verify the returns? Can you or your advisors speak to other investors in their previous deals?

- Evaluate the Promoter/Operator II: Reputation – How long have you known them? What is their reputation? Call their references and obtain a list of all deals that they have done and ask for those references. You want to guard against select references. Also, have your attorney run a check on lawsuits that the operator is involved or has been involved in over the years.

- How were the projections determined? Ask your accountant to verify. Are they making assumptions out of blue sky or are the assumptions thorough and grounded in reality?

- Does the venture have financing in place? If not, why not?

- For your investment, are you receiving a prorata portion of the profits or is the promoter receiving a percentage of the profits without investing cash? Sometimes that is acceptable, but it must be an equitable percentage.

- How much of the promoter's money are they putting in the venture?

- How much are the other partners putting in the venture? Does their percentage ownership and division of the profits match yours?

- How is the promoter manager being compensated and is the fee fair market? You want to avoid someone looking for you to fund their lifestyle. See above regarding Hedge Funds.

- Do you and the other partners have the right to call for a third-party audit? Can they remove the manager for cause? Is the management agreement evergreen (forever) or does it have a term?

- Are you the deep pocket in the venture? Are you obligated to sign for any debt? If so, you must be sure that you do not sign a loan that requires joint and several liability making you liable for all the debt. This is why your attorney is essential, but you must also be aware of this. Just because you are told you are not liable, that does not mean that the documents will state the same thing.

- What are your obligations in the event that the venture loses money? Are you obligated if there is a cash call to put more money in? Failing to do so and being diluted is much better than throwing good money after bad.

- Do you know the partners in the venture? This is one of the most important things to evaluate.

- Are related party transactions allowed? This is an area where investors can get hurt. For example, an oil well deal that is set up with the promoter receiving 20% and the investors receiving 80% of the profits. Even though the well is producing, the promoter owns a maintenance company and charges other expenses to the venture resulting in little or no cash flow. While this may be unethical, if the agreement allows the operator to do this, there is little that can be done.

- How do you get out of the venture? Can you sell your shares or is this restricted? What happens upon your death or disability?

- Are there non-competition provisions in the agreement and if so, do they apply to you?

Chapter 10 - The Role of Alternative Investments & Evaluating Ancillary Deals

- Lastly, is this a business you understand? Generally, either become a student of the business or stick with something you know and can control, such as a medical office building with your practice partners. Your chances of success rise considerably.

"The less you bet, the more you lose when you win." This quote is attributed to Wyatt Earp, the famous sheriff, gunfighter, and gambler who ran a faro (the 19th century version of baccarat) game in Tombstone, Arizona. Wyatt had the house edge so, of course he would have said this. Ancillary ventures have a place in your portfolio but be careful and use your Tribe to advise you. As with many things, it is better to do business with people you know, but more importantly, with a business that you understand. Oil wells, hamster balls and goldmines are very different than practicing medicine. There are charlatans out there but there are also very good operators. Do your homework and find the good ones.

Chapter XI
Conclusion

It is my hope that this book provides a valuable contribution for medical students, physicians, and others in healthcare. The practice of medicine is a noble profession, and it is not fair that you are expected to understand the ins and outs of business, finance, the law, and the lessons learned through the school of hard knocks. The purpose of this book is to provide you a foundation in personal finance so you don't make the mistakes that so many others do, give you a clear path to find success as an investor and avoid the investing pitfalls that so many succumb to and finally, to emphasize that personal success is a function of connecting with people, being a light for them, and encouraging them. Build a team around you because the more people you like, the happier you will be.

This book was a pleasure to write, and your feedback and thoughts are always welcome. Please feel free to reach out to me with questions, suggestions, and comments.

About the Author

Joseph S Zasa, JD

Joe Zasa is the Co-Founder and Managing Partner of ASD Management; an operator of ambulatory surgery centers (ASCs) throughout the United States. Founded in 1996, ASD Management's focus is on existing surgery centers that require turnaround expertise, development of new surgery centers with physicians and hospitals, and management of the firms' ASCs.

Joe is the author of <u>Developing and Managing Surgery Centers</u>, the first comprehensive book on ASC management published in 2016 and a five-star rated publication on Amazon.com. It is in its 3rd edition and is co-published by the Ambulatory Surgery Center Association. He is also a full-time faculty member at the University of Alabama Birmingham School of Health Sciences where he teaches surgery center management to the Master of Health Administration students and the University of Alabama Heersink School of Medicine where he teaches medical students business principles and financial literacy.

Mr. Zasa received his Juris Doctorate from Washington and Lee University, and his bachelor's degree from the University of Alabama.

He can be reached through his website at www.asdmanagement.com or his email at joezasa@asdmanagement.com

Appendix I
Should We Be Tactical?
By Elisabetta Basilico, PhD, CFA, and Preston McSwain
December 20, 2021

All want to add value in their various endeavors, and many offer ideas on how to enhance results. This is true in almost everything we consume – a better way to work out or a twist on a classic recipe.

In the investment world, arguably the most famous work done on what adds value to total portfolio performance was conducted by Brinson, Hood, and Beebower, which they detailed in a 1991 paper titled, <u>Determinants of Portfolio Performance</u>. The team of researchers developed what has become the generally accepted framework on how to evaluate what drives investment performance, articulating the following three key activities that an investor, manager, or allocator can employ:

1. Strategic Long-Term Asset Allocation – Establishing Investment Policy Statements (IPS) that set long-term targets for each asset class (equities, bonds, etc.)

2. Tactical Asset Allocation – Market timing decisions that deviate from long-term IPS targets and tilt allocations to overweight or underweight an asset class

Appendix I

3. Manager Selection – Employing a process that strives to find managers that can outperform markets or asset classes and tactically implement or make changes among them at the correct time (picking so-called active managers)

A new paper is now out about number two, and we will touch on number one at the end.

Before we do, however, let's briefly revisit number three – what the evidence says about investment professionals' ability to select managers at the correct time, who can outperform the market going forward.

In 2019, we published an article asking this question: <u>Are Selectors Good at Selecting?</u>

Our paper was based on an in-depth study conducted by researchers from the Sand Business School at the University of Oxford, with assistance from leading finance figures at MIT, and data from well-respected firms such as eVestment and Greenwich Associates. In addition, we touched on work from Finance Departments at St. John's University and New York University.

What did these peer-reviewed research studies show – have leading industry professionals and well-resourced and focused teams been able to find outperforming strategies?

As we wrote, unfortunately, for many of us who have worked in the field for many years, the answer is brutal:

"No"

After analyzing the recommendations of investment consultants, who represented 90% of the institutional U.S. manager selection market, researchers found no statistically significant evidence that their fund recommendations outperformed.

In addition, fund selection teams inside large investment management firms were found to pick funds that consistently and significantly underperform.

Appendix I

Throwing even more doubt on the ability of any of us to be able to find outliers at the correct time, last year we highlighted more research in a piece we titled <u>Trillions of Influence</u>, which investigated whether the influencers of finance (global institutional investors) are good at selecting top managers.

The answer was also tough for many to take.

"No."

This, <u>and other industry research</u>, continues to strongly suggest that manager selection activities continue to be what Charles Ellis, the founder of the global manager analysis firm Greenwich Associates, and long-time head of Yale's Investment Committee, has called a Loser's Game.

A recent paper titled, <u>Is Tactical Allocation a Winning Strategy?</u>, allows us to now comment on number two – the ability of professionals to add value by tactically tilting a portfolio away from long-term IPS allocation targets.

Researchers looked at the performance of institutional quality funds run by investment firms who use a multitude of resources and processes to assess the attractiveness of various asset classes and change their weights in portfolios – what are called Tactical Asset Allocation (TAA) Funds.

After analyzing the risk-adjusted returns of over 100 TAA strategies, looking at Sharpe and Sortino ratios as compared to a number of domestic and international benchmarks, the study found that TAA funds have underperformed over long-term periods and that statistically, this was not due to chance.

Some suggest that tactical moves are indeed difficult to implement in bull markets but say that a TAA approach helps protect portfolios in bear markets and adds value during a financial crisis.

Unfortunately, again, this is not what the research showed when looking at the actual performance of TAA funds.

To try to find out if fees were the reason for underperformance (a TAA approach can be expensive – average costs were found to be 1.4% per year as a percentage of assets under management), they also analyzed the performance of TAA funds gross of fees. As before, the research found no evidence of outperformance or Alpha.

As with the manager selection studies we reviewed, the results from this analysis of TAA strategies have been confirmed by other academic papers, such as one titled, Static Indexing Beats Asset Allocation. The title does not bury the lead, as researchers from Duke University found the following:

- High Fees and Taxes – TAA funds are more expensive and have higher turnover, which can make them less tax-efficient

- Underperformance – TAA funds underperform long-term static IPS driven index strategies, significantly, ranging between approximately 2-5% per year.

This all brings us back to the start and number one on our list – the value of setting long-term IPS asset allocation targets and sticking to them, what we have called The Simple Alternative.

Many suggest that the so-called Brinson study said that more than 90% of performance comes from asset allocation decisions.

We understand why this is suggested, as many tout an ability to add value with their asset allocation process. This, however, is not what Brinson and his fellow researchers were really saying.

The study suggested that, after looking at the performance of a sizable sample of large, well-resourced institutional investment funds, the evidence at the time showed that active decisions related to tactical asset allocation and manager selection did little to improve performance.

As more and more data has arrived and better analytical tools have been developed, we continue to find similar things – active investment decisions do not seem to add much value. In contrast, they seem to increase the probability of underperforming.

In saying all of this, we are not suggesting that we should ignore significant events that do happen or not keep an eye out for unique opportunities. We should.

Based on the continued evidence, however, we should also be open and humble about our ability to outperform the broad market.

The probability of adding value through tactical asset allocation or manager selection decisions is very low, as the probability of getting it wrong is very high.

Related Reading:

Outperformance in Down Markets 100% of the Time? – FWP

How to Actively Add Value – Research Roundtable

What Would Yale Do If It Was Taxable? – Trust & Estates

What Needs to Change? – Research Roundtable

Appendix II
An Interview with Robin Wigglesworth about Index Funds

The following is an excerpt from an interview conducted by Preston McSwain with Robin Wigglesworth from the Financial Times about his new book detailing the history and success of index investing.

Trillions – Our Talk With Robin Wigglesworth About Index Funds

By Preston McSwain, January 4, 2022

A raft of articles and books have been written about index funds.

However, there are few pieces that explain how the idea of tracking an investment market started and all that happened along the way.

Trillions, written by Robin Wigglesworth, a well-known writer for the Financial Times, does all of this and more, bringing the quantitative evidence behind the index fund to life, with great stories about its history and the people that drove its success.

I reached out to Robin in the hope that he would spend a little time

Appendix II

talking with me about his book. Robin was generous enough to speak with me for well over an hour on Zoom, late into the evening his time in Norway.

The summary of our talk below has been edited for clarity. It might be what the FT calls a Long Read, but I think you will find it interesting and insightful. I thoroughly enjoyed our talk and learned a great deal reading Robin's book. If anyone would like a copy of Trillions, please let me know and I will send you one.

Preston: Trillions covers many different aspects of index investing, from the original ideas behind it, how it got started, and how indexing has grown to where it is today.

How did you decide to focus on this topic?

Robin: Index fund investing can come across as fairly boring. When you do a deeper dive, though, it has shaken up pretty much everything in the financial industry and I felt the ideas behind it were not well covered.

I'm a history buff, so I also wanted to tell a story about how the investment industry has evolved over the past hundred years through the prism of index funds.

This humble, unassuming, unlikely protagonist – the index fund – was widely derided at its birth. But it has grown and hammered all of the people that used to make fun of it.

I try to tell a broader history about investing… how the idea of index fund invested started and then how it evolved.

I felt it was unfair to dump readers in 19th century France so, I started the book about a big bet – one between Warren Buffett and Protйgй Partners.

The stakes were high and I thought it was a fun, cinematic way to explain what a hedge fund is as compared to an index fund.

Preston: Maybe something of a classic tortoise and hare race. An active manager that aggressively strives to outperform the market versus a manager that strives to track the performance of the overall market in a manner that may seem passive.

Robin: Yes. The bet from the head of Protйgй Partners, Ted Seides, was that top hedge funds, selected by a well-resourced and seasoned manager selection team, would outperform an index fund designed to track the S&P500 over a 10-year period.

Buffett took the other side, that an S&P 500 index fund would outperform top hedge funds.

And…

Warren won – Big.

Preston: It did indeed get a lot of press and maybe changed some opinions about indexing.

Robin: Yes – Again.

A problem with the bet is that, even if Seides had won, I don't think it would have changed the fundamental data or the fundamental arguments in favor of indexing.

Preston: You mentioned 19th century France.

I've been in the investment business for the better part of 30 years, but I had never heard about the work of Louis Bachelier or that the evidence in support of indexing started in the late 1800s.

Tell us more about this – what did his research show?

Robin: I have a soft spot for Bachelier, as he died in obscurity, only much later to be recognized for his genius.

He was not necessarily interested in finance. Bachelier was a mathematician.

While working a part time job at the Paris Stock Exchange, though, he became interested in trying to decode the price fluctuations of stock prices. He became fascinated by it and ultimately, he wrote his Ph.D. thesis on the movements of the market.

Bachelier quantified for the first time how stocks moved randomly – what Burton Malkiel famously coined a Random Walk. He is really a godfather of efficient markets.

Preston: Next, you mention Jimmy Savage. If it hadn't been for him, and a somewhat random discovery of Bachelier's Ph.D. thesis, would indexing be where it is today?

Robin: Jimmy Savage, whom Milton Friedman described as "one of the few people I have met whom I would unhesitatingly call a genius," literally discovered Bachelier's Ph.D. thesis by chance.

Savage happened to be best buddies with the Nobel Prize winner Paul Samuelson and sent him a post card literally asking if he had "ever heard of this guy," saying that "Bachelier seems to have had something of a one-track mind. But what a track!"

Separately, Bachelier's work then got to a young grad, Eugene Fama, who also went on to win the Nobel Prize, based on his further quantification of how low the probability of anyone being able to predict the price movements of stocks really is.

It is more complex than you can manage in a book narrative, but it was fascinating seeing how the idea spread.

Preston: As you wrote, Bachelier's work "helped explain one of the most puzzling aspects of the investment industry – why most professional money managers seemed to do such an abysmal job."

Next, you mention Alfred Cowles, III, who also dove deep into financial data in an attempt to improve the way his family managed money.

Robin: Cowles was a relentless measurer. He'd count the average height of people that he met and loved counting or measuring everything in the stock market.

He was born into wealth, as an heir to the Chicago Tribune fortune, but he was struck with tuberculosis in the 1920s.

Cowles was sent to Colorado to recover and, while there, with more time on his hands, he took over the management of the family fortune.

When the Great Depression happened, he was shocked to discover that all the newsletters and research reports he subscribed to were useless.

To try to get to the bottom of why, as far as I can tell, he put together the first comprehensive study of how well professionals predicted the stock market.

Cowles went through everything. He analyzed the track records of leading insurance companies (some of the largest professional investors of that time), dozens of investor publications (the research reports of today), and Dow Theory, which was first espoused by Wall Street Journal founder, Charles Dow.

His findings were published in a 1932 paper titled, <u>Can Stock Market Forecasters Forecast?</u>

Cowles summed up the results of this study in a three-word abstract:

"It is doubtful."

He basically ended up finding that the industry was turning out a lot of chaff and not a lot of wheat.

Preston: And, as you also mentioned, IBM reached similar conclusions in the 1940s, when they used early computing systems to analyze approximately 7,000 investment forecasts.

Robin: The story of indexing tracks the dawn of the computer age quite well, because people, with computers, could do type of analysis required to verify how well investors had performed.

The real Genesis moment in the eyes of many was the work done by the Center for Research in Security Prices (CRSP) in the early 1960s

Appendix II

that was commissioned by Merrill Lynch.

Merrill wanted to sell stocks to ordinary Americans, but the SEC prevented them from running ads promoting stocks, saying that they needed to prove that stocks were a good long-term investment.

To make their case to the SEC, Merrill hired Jim Lorie, a professor at Chicago, and his colleague Larry Fisher, to crunch the data.

To help make the case, though, they first had to find out what the total returns of stocks had actually been – something that had never been accurately quantified.

After spending four years creating a database that covered decades worth of old journals, Lorie and Fisher found that the long-term return of the U.S. stock market had been about 9% per year.

Merrill Lynch was pleased and, based on this return, the SEC allowed them to print their ad.

It was very successful and powered Merrill's Thundering Herd of stock sales professionals across America.

Problematically for the investment industry, however, was the 9% annualized number – not far off what is still the long-term average yearly return for stocks in the U.S.1.

Lorie and Fisher found that return of the market as a whole was quite a lot higher than the average returns of professional investors.

Preston: Even though it was commissioned by the industry, they got back something that they might not have wanted – that their promoted stock picking might not be adding much value?

Robin: I'm sure they edited that part of it.

Preston: One of my biggest take-aways from your book is this:

Since 1900, we have been crunching the numbers and data.

And...

Appendix II

Every time we have analyzed numbers, each time with better and better databases and systems, we get the same conclusions – most professional investors don't beat the market.

Robin: I think the conclusions started coming even before we had the data.

Fred Schwed famously wrote <u>Where Are The Customers' Yachts?</u> in 1940, right?

There was an understanding after the South Sea bubble, the Mississippi bubble, the Great Depression, when investment trusts were stripped of all of their infallibility…

That… professional investors weren't actually that good.

People are really good at ignoring inconvenient truths, though, and before the internet, it was a lot easier.

Data started being complied in the 1930s by people like Cowles. In the 1960s, computers then allowed things to all come together.

I wouldn't say in an irrefutable way by then, but pretty comprehensively.

Preston: In spite of all the building evidence, though, you write about how, without the dogged support of the Chairman of Wells Fargo, index funds might have never really gotten off the ground.

Robin: In a paradox, we think of the 1970s as an era of wasteful CEOs spending.

But without a pet project, run by John McQuown, that was funded by two separate heads of Wells Fargo, index funds might not be what they are today.

With somewhat of an unlimited budget, and losses that lasted for about 20 years, McQuown was able to build what was probably the biggest collection of big investment brains that has ever been assembled.

Appendix II

I call it the Manhattan Project of Finance, that at various points included Bill Sharpe, James Lorie, Lawrence Fisher, Michael Jensen, Harry Markowitz, Merton Miller, Jack Treynor, Fischer Black, and Myron Scholes.

They worked on many things like FICO scores and what eventually became MasterCard.

But...

I believe that the index fund was the greatest invention of them all.

In spite of significant initial opposition from the stock pickers inside the Wells Fargo Trust Department, it eventually morphed into Wells Fargo Investment Advisors, which then became Barclays Global investors, and finally Blackrock, the world's biggest investment company.

This pet project revolutionized the investment world and I'd argue was the start of quantitative investing.

Preston: You just mentioned something I've thought a lot about over my career.

My first job in money management was at State Street Asset Management, what is now called SSGA, the home of many large index ETFs such as SPY.

As you mention in your book about Wells Fargo, we had two different floors.

One was the Trust Department, which managed money in a fashion that is now called active management.

Index mutual funds and ETFs didn't really exist at scale at the time, but on my floor, we managed sizable index tracking strategies for large pension funds, employing many math majors, PhDs, and CFAs, who actively worked to develop quantitative models to manage money.

Fast forward to now, even though I could argue that the index floor was much more active than the Trust Company floor, we would call the Trust Company floor active and the index floor passive.

How did this come to be?

Robin: The line between active and passive is certainly arbitrary and gets blurred all the time.

The way I see it is sort of an axis of systematic versus discretionary.

Index fund investors were the first systematic investors – the genesis of quant investing.

Index investing is just one facet of quant investing – the biggest one, but just one.

A lot of the people that invented index funds were not efficient market zealots. They were just trying to develop strategies that were able to achieve the performance of the market as a whole.

Based on what the quantitative studies were showing, if they could do this, they believed they would be able to produce better performance.

Preston: When selecting an investment manager, I argue that you want to find a manager that is extraordinarily process driven, has high rigor and, following the data, constructs portfolios in a systematic way.

Along these lines, is there really much difference between good index management and good active management?

Robin: Today there's a widespread recognition that the best active managers are not the iconoclastic geniuses.

They might be geniuses and they might be iconoclastic, but you want someone that has a repeatable process.

The idea of being able to find a great person, entrusting it to this great person until they lose their touch, and then searching for another one, has come under question.

With measurement, we've come to realize that many investment managers have just delivered the returns of the market, or a segment of it, minus their costs.

Over the past fifty years, I think there has been a greater realization that a lot of what the better active managers do can be quantitatively systematized and packaged up more cheaply.

You could argue that Ben Graham was the original quant, because he was a very rigorous person. He liked numbers. He liked measuring things and believed in a rigorous scientific approach to investing, which was actually anathema at the time.

Preston: Graham is also often called the father of value investing.

Tying this back to the story of indexing, do you think it would exist at the scale it does today if it were not for another maybe random event…

The long stretch of value underperformance in the late 1960s, which led to the rise of the so-called aggressive growth Whiz Kids in Boston, such as Nick Thorndike, who took over an old line value firm in Philadelphia, Wellington Management.

Robin: That's a good question.

Without Thorndike, his partners, and their growth fund, there probably wouldn't have been a Vanguard.

Turning the clock back, Bogle was hotshot young executive at Wellington and was given the reins in the 1960 to run the firm. Unfortunately for him, this was maybe the first growth bubble and Wellington's conservative value management style wasn't considered to be cool anymore.

In an effort to reinvigorate the firm, Jack decided to merge Wellington with the go-go era Boston manager you mentioned, Thorndike, Doran, Paine, Lewis & Doran.

Everything worked fine to start but, as we know, nothing raises tensions as much as a nasty bear market, and after the large market drop in the 1970s, Jack got sacked.

Connecting on a Hail Mary pass to try to stay in the investment business, Jack was able set up a new firm originally owned by the Wellington Funds that would do administrative work for the funds.

Though a loophole that Jack created, a more computer driven form of investing that he also proposed was considered to be administrative, so was allowed to be done as it was not deemed to be competitive to Wellington.

It eventually all came together and, with a grandiose name that Jack coined, Vanguard's index fund management started.

I think indexing would definitely be here but, without the zeal to succeed that Bogle brought to it, I don't think it would be where it is today.

Appendix III
A Primer on Legal Issues

By Amber Walsh, Esq. and Scott Becker, Esq.

Reprinted from <u>Developing and Managing Surgery Centers</u> by Joseph S. Zasa and Robert J. Zasa

The following is reprinted from my first book and is very relevant for physicians and healthcare professionals. While it is specific to that book's main topic centering on ambulatory surgery centers (ASCs), the regulatory analysis is very applicable for physicians regardless of their involvement in ASCs or other ancillary ventures because the federal Anti-Kickback Statute applies to all forms of healthcare and some knowledge of it must be understood by physicians due to the high incidence of actions against physicians under this act.

Anti-Kickback Issues

ASCs that bill and collect from Medicare, Medicaid or other government programs are subject to the federal Anti-Kickback Statute, which prohibits the knowing and willful offer, payment, solicitation, or receipt of any sort of remuneration in exchange for the referral of any service potentially reimbursable under such healthcare programs. It is an intent-based statute, meaning the intention of the parties in entering into a particular arrangement, including structuring ownership of an ASC, will be examined in order to determine the appropriateness of an arrangement.

Over the last few years, the federal government has allocated huge increases in funds for health care fraud enforcement, with a 2015 budget for the US Department of Health and Human Services (HHS) of $2.0 billion. This enforcement focuses on billing and collections, as well as physician-hospital and physician-provider relationships. Further, there has been a huge increase in false claims cases in all health care sectors, with recoveries for health care fraud in 2014 reaching $2.3 billion in federal losses alone.

In the past, fraud enforcement focused heavily on billing and collections. Now, significant fraud and abuse resources are being put toward review of different types of arrangements between all types of providers and physicians who refer them, and their compliance with the Stark Law and Federal Anti-Kickback Statute. Specifically, a lot of review surrounds whether or not the particular arrangement meets a Safe Harbor to the Anti-Kickback Statute.

There has been an evolution of different types of possible relationships under scrutiny. These include situations where parties are trying to sell shares to physicians at prices that may be below fair market value, situations where facilities are leasing equipment on a per-click basis from physicians, and situations where parties want to sell different quantities of shares to different physicians or pay different types of questionable medical director fees to different physicians.

As the government allocates more money to anti-fraud initiatives, it is important to keep an eye on what types of activities surgery centers are engaging in and what types of activities the government is particularly targeting.

Safe Harbors, noncompliant physicians: The HHS Office of Inspector General (the OIG) published Safe Harbor regulations describing certain investment and compensation arrangements that the OIG has determined involve minimal opportunity for abuse. So long as every element of a particular Safe Harbor is satisfied, the arrangement will be automatically deemed compliant with the Anti-Kickback Statute. However, an arrangement that meets many but not all elements of a Safe Harbor may still be compliant with the Anti-Kickback Statute, although its lack of Safe Harbor immunity makes it subject to potential scrutiny. In particular, there are four separate Safe Harbors for ASC investment models that are similar in nature and are generally grouped together and referred to as the "ASC Safe Harbor." A core concern the OIG articulated in the development of the ASC Safe Harbor was with indirect referrals and that distributions from an ASC could be a disguised reward to physicians for referrals where the referring physicians do not perform the services themselves. Therefore, among other qualitative elements, there are two key quantitate elements of the ASC Safe Harbor as follows:

The physician derives at least 1/3 of his or her annual medical practice income (from all sources) from performing surgical procedures on the list of Medicare ASC-eligible procedures.

In the case of a multi-specialty center, the physician performs at least 1/3 of his or her own ASC-eligible procedures at the applicable center.

Over the past few years, parties have become more aggressive in trying to redeem physicians who are not Safe Harbor compliant as existing physicians are increasingly less patient with non-Safe Harbor compliant physicians. See 42 C.F.R. § 1001.952 (2014). In some instances, because a physician's particular situation may make his or her noncompliance less risky for the center (for example, if the physician does not serve as a referral source to the center, the purpose of his or her investment was not to reward or induce referrals, etc.), depending on the circumstances, such redemptions can be seen as punitive and tied to referrals, creating Anti-Kickback risk.

In many situations to reduce the risk of litigation related to such redemptions, the parties may offer the noncompliant physician's full value for the shares, even though the full value is not required under the surgery center's operating agreement. The parties may also give the noncompliant physicians a long notice period for coming into compliance with the Safe Harbor.

It is important that Safe Harbor concepts generally not be applied in a discriminatory manner. Rather, the Safe Harbor elements should be consistently applied to all physician members to use them as enforcement and for redeeming physicians. It is critical that redemption be truly based on a desire for the center to be compliant with the Safe Harbor rather than for revenue generating purposes (there has been increase litigation in this area). Further, there is at least one significant case the use of the Safe Harbor elements was successfully challenged by a physician.

Safe Harbors, indirect referrals: The government continues to express great discomfort with indirect referral sources and noncompliant physicians. That said, the government is very cautiously but intelligently handling cross-referral relationships as evidenced by the extreme caution exercised by the Office of Inspector General (OIG) of HHS issuing a positive advisory opinion to a hospital-physician joint venture where only a small number of the orthopedic physicians were not Safe Harbor compliant (4 of the 18 physicians were not compliant) but were potential referral sources. There, in fact, the OIG prohibited the referral of cases from the noncompliant physicians to parties that would receive such referrals and then use the surgery center for those cases. In reaching its conclusion, the OIG said:

In the circumstances presented, notwithstanding that those 4 inpatient surgeons will not regularly practice at the ASC, we conclude the ASC is unlikely to be a vehicle for them to profit from referrals. The Requestors have certified that, as practitioners of subspecialties of orthopedic surgery that require a hospital operating room setting, the inpatient surgeons rarely have occasion to refer patients for ASC-Qualified Procedures (other than pain management procedures discussed below). Moreover, like the other surgeon investors, the inpatient surgeons are regularly engaged in a genuine surgical practice, deriving at least 1/3 of their medical practice income from procedures requiring a hospital operating room setting. The inpatient surgeons are qualified to perform surgeries at the ASC and may choose to do so (and earn the professional fees) in medically appropriate cases. Also, the inpatient surgeons comprise a small proportion of the surgeon investors, a majority of who will use the ASC on a regular basis as part of their medical practice. This arrangement is readily distinguishable from potentially riskier arrangements in which few investing physicians actually use the ASC on a regular basis or in which investing physicians are significant potential referral sources for other investors or the ASC, as when primary care physicians invest in a surgical ASC or cardiologists invest in a cardiac surgery ASC.

Here, the arrangement did not meet every requirement of the Safe Harbor. However, certain other factors, such as the infrequency of the inpatient surgeons referring patients for ASC-eligible procedures, led the OIG to conclude that, although the arrangement posed some risk, the safeguards put in place by the parties sufficiently reduced the risk of illegal kickbacks to warrant granting the positive advisory opinion.

Buy-in Pricing for New Physicians

ASCs continue to look for ways to reduce buy-in amounts for physicians. Increasingly, there are arguments for lower valuations based on the impact of the changing economy on surgery centers and the uncertainty of profits going forward. But of course, the price for shares must remain fair market value. In order to make share pricing more manageable, it is also possible for junior physicians to buy fewer shares, to obtain loans from companies in the business of providing financing for physician buy-ins (provided such buy-ins are not guaranteed by any other investor or the surgery center) and to engage in opportunities like recapitalizations to further reduce the cost and value of the center. Again, a key issue is ensuring the center is not selling shares to physicians at below fair market value to induce the referral of cases or the retention for cases.

Can a partner physician be redeemed? One question closely tied to

Safe Harbor is, "Can I kill a physician who does not perform cases at the center?" The answer, briefly stated, is you cannot kill such a physician. However, there are possibilities to work with the Safe Harbor and compliance guidelines to see if the physician is someone that should be redeemed pursuant to not complying with the Safe Harbor or other operating agreement terms. There has been increased litigation in this area.

Sale of additional shares to highly productive physicians:

There are often situations where a physician producing surgical volume proportionately higher than other owners wants to buy additional shares. In general, to facilitate such a request poses Anti-Kickback Statute risk. It is possible for that physician to try to buy additional shares from other partners. The other partners cannot sell their shares to the high producing physician simply to help keep his or her cases at the center. If existing partners want to sell shares, for reasons unrelated to retaining volume, it is not illegal for them to sell shares to high producing physicians. The sale of shares should be at fair market value.

Profiting from anesthesia and pathology:

Increasingly, there are situations where centers and physicians are looking for ways to profit from ancillary services such as anesthesia, pathology or other areas. Again, there are certain ways in which an ASC can lawfully profit from anesthesia in a legal manner. However, there are certain other structures, which are of more significant concern with respect to the legality of profiting from anesthesia.

This area has come under attack by the American Society of Anesthesiology and was the subject of OIG Advisory Opinion 12-06. This Advisory Opinion concerns two fact patterns, both of which relate to an ASC's relationship with its anesthesia provider. The first created an arrangement where the anesthesia provider would continue to serve as the centers' exclusive provider of anesthesia services and bill and retain all collections from patients and third-party payers, including Medicare, for its services. OIG did not offer a favorable advisory opinion to this arrangement because OIG's view was that it essentially paid the ASC twice for the same services, and the additional remuneration paid by the anesthesia provider in the form of management services fees could unduly influence the ASC to select the anesthesia provider as the ASC's exclusive provider.

The second fact pattern created separate companies for the purpose of providing anesthesia-related services to outpatients undergoing surgery at the center. The concern there was that the ASC was forcing an anesthesia group to provide remuneration to the ASC in exchange for an exclusive anesthesia agreement. OIG determined that many of the elements of suspect arrangements were present in the proposed arrangements. These elements included that the ASC's physician owners (1) would be expanding into a related line of business (anesthesia services) that would be wholly dependent on the ASC's referrals, (2) would not actually operate the subsidiaries, but would contract out the operations exclusively to the anesthesia group, and (3) would have minimal business risk because they would control the amount of business, they would refer to the subsidiaries.

The laws with respect to profiting from pathology are somewhat murkier. There is often ability for gastroenterology practices related to surgery centers to perform pathology services in their own office and profit from these services at the practical level. However, there is a whole range of analysis that has to be performed to ensure that such efforts (namely the relationship between the ASC and the practice) comply with the Anti-Kickback Statute, the Stark Act, and the Anti-Markup Provisions.

Per-click Relationships

There have traditionally been several different types of "per-click" arrangements between ASCs and third-party providers (including physician owners) for such items as gamma knives, lithotripters, lasers, CT and MRI scanners and other types of equipment. However, the government has expressed negative opinions about such arrangements and parties should be quite cautious regarding the use of per-click arrangements. CMS explained its position in the commentary to the Stark Law rules regarding such arrangements. And, although the Stark Law is generally not applicable to ASCs, this insight into mindset of the government is illustrative:

At this time, we are adopting our proposal to prohibit per-click payments to physician lessors for services rendered to patients who were referred by the physician lessor. We continue to have concerns that such arrangements are susceptible to abuse, and we also rely on our authority under sections 1877(e)(1)(A)(vi) and 1877(e)(l)(B)(vi) of the Act to disallow them ...

We are also taking this opportunity to remind parties to per-use leasing arrangements that the existing exceptions include the requirements that the leasing agreement be at fair market value (§411.357(a)(4) and §411.357(b)(4)) and that it be commercially reasonable even if no referrals were made between the parties (§411.357(a)(6) and §411.357(b)(5)).

For example, we do not consider an agreement to be at fair market value if the lessee is paying a physician substantially more for a lithotripter or other equipment and a technologist than it would have to pay a non-physician owned company for the same or similar equipment and service. As a further example, we would also have a serious question as to whether an agreement is commercially reasonable if the lessee is performing a sufficiently high volume of procedures, such that it would be economically feasible to purchase the equipment rather than continuing to lease it from a physician or physician entity that refers patients to the lessee for DHS. Such agreements raise the questions of whether the lessee is paying the lessor more than what it would have to pay another lessor, or is leasing equipment rather than purchasing it, because the lessee wishes to reward the lessor for referrals and/ or because it is concerned that, absent such a leasing arrangement, referrals from the lessor would cease. In some cases, depending on the circumstances, such arrangements may also implicate the anti-kickback statute.

Although the statements issued above largely relate to non-ASC services, these same fair market value and remuneration concerns and rewards for referrals are prevalent in the anti-kickback analysis for

ASCs as well. Overall, if an ASC is considering a per-click arrangement, it should carefully consider whether such an arrangement is commercially reasonable after all referrals are removed from the analysis; that is, is it based on referrals or is it a cost-effective way to obtain the equipment.

Medical Directorships

Medical directorships should be used only if the medical director is providing true medical director and clinical administrative services needed by the center. If a typical center has one medical director who is an anesthesiologist and/or another surgeon truly involved in directorship activities, that should be the core model a surgery center should consider. When looking at other situations, for example, such as having a medical director for each specialty, there must be a legitimate reason for the need for multiple medical directors, and any fees paid for directorships must be fair market value. Such arrangement must not be intended to provide a kickback in exchange for cases.

Increasingly, there are situations where physicians buy intraocular lenses (IOL), specifically the premium lenses, and sell them to their patients. Here, the physicians may or may not buy these lenses from the surgery center itself and some physicians may have a relationship where they directly buy the lenses and sell them to patients. Either way, these transactions raise issues as to how much money goes back and forth between the surgery center and the physicians as to the IOLs and whether the surgery center is improperly allowing the physician at the center to profit from the sale of equipment and supplies. There are also issues as to the proper pricing of such lenses sold to patients. There could also be situations where two lens manufactures may provide free sample lenses to physicians and the physicians may sell these lenses to patients. These situations create material risk under the Anti- Kickback Statute, other federal laws and potentially state law as well.

Physician Owned Equipment and Supplies Companies

One of the interesting newer scenarios is where physicians own an equipment or supplies company and sell goods to the surgery center. In essence, the physicians become a middleman between the surgery center and the manufacturer. This allows the physicians to profit on the sale of equipment or supplies used in any cases that they perform. ASCs should generally be cautious regarding these relationships. OIG has stated its concerns with physician-owned entities when it wrote "the financial incentives [Physician Owned Distributorships (PODs)] offer to their physician-owners may induce the physicians both to perform more procedures (or more extensive procedures) than are medically necessary and to use the devices the PODs sell in lieu of other, potentially more clinically appropriate devices."

HOPD Transactions and Co-management Deals

There has been substantial growth in situations in which a surgery center is sold to a hospital and the hospital then operates the ASC as a hospital department and develops what is titled a "co-management" relationship. This provides the physician or physician group compensation for managing the service of the hospital-purchased ASC which becomes a hospital outpatient department (known as an HOPD) but allows the hospital to really be the owner and provider of the services and to provide the services at hospital outpatient department rates.

The great challenge in these relationships is often assuring that they are fair market value and that physicians are being paid for reasonably needed services and not just a means to get money to physicians in exchange for business. The further great challenge of these relationships will be how they look 3 to 5 years after a transaction is completed. In essence, there is nothing as congruent in terms of interests as a true joint venture. Over time, there is great likelihood case volumes will be reduced and that the glue of the relationship will be not as strong as it was when first formed. On occasion, OIG has approved of such arrangements, and based on an analysis of the specific facts and circumstances, OIG has noted:

Properly structured, arrangements that compensate physicians for achieving hospital cost savings can serve legitimate business and medical purposes. Specifically, properly structured arrangements may increase efficiency and reduce waste, thereby potentially increasing a hospital's profitability. However, such arrangements can potentially influence physician judgment to the detriment of patient care. Our concerns include, but are not limited to, the following: (i) stinting on patient care, (ii) "cherry picking" healthy patients and steering sicker (and more costly) patients to hospitals that do not offer such arrangements, (iii) payments to induce patient referrals, and (iv) unfair competition among hospitals offering incentive compensation programs to foster physician loyalty and to attract more referrals.

Out-of-Network Reimbursement

The ability to profit substantially from out-of-network patients continues to decrease. Payers are increasingly aggressive regarding recoupment, collection of appropriate co-payments from patients and increasing co-payment and deductible responsibilities. Thus, the ability to make outsized profits or have serious negotiation leverage through the use of out-of-network continues to be hampered.

On the out-of-network side, increasingly there are situations where payers either issue audit letters to surgery centers, develop no-pay policies on out-of-network, or pay surgery centers just a fraction of what they expect to get paid. Surgery centers, on their end, are increasingly making efforts to work with state departments of insurance to explain how the cutting off of out-of-network precludes patients from accessing true Preferred Provider Organization (PPO) benefits. There is a handful of cases that discuss whether or not payers have responsibilities to pay providers when providers are serving patients out-of-network and in some situations reducing co-payments. This is an evolving area that continues to become more combative.

Joint Venture Managed Care Contracting

There are two antitrust issues that are most prevalent in the ASC industry. First, there is a question as to whether a hospital and physicians can jointly contract to try to obtain better rates from managed care payers. Here, the key issue is ensuring that two entities can be considered one entity for purposes of the antitrust laws, which makes them legally incapable of conspiring with each other. There is a significant difference in legal interpretations on this across the country. For example, if a hospital owns 80 percent or more of the surgery center and has substantial control of the surgery center, there are very strong arguments that conspiring together is not possible from an antitrust law perspective (that is, the hospital and surgery center are one). When the ownership is between 50 percent and 80 percent, the determination differs from district court to district court, which is to say by region of the country. Further, the amount of control the hospital has over the surgery center is a critical component of the ultimate determination. Where a hospital owns less than 50 percent of the surgery center, it may still be possible for the hospital and surgery center to be considered one entity, but the hospital must have very substantial control of the surgery center.

Another common antitrust issue arises when a surgery center is excluded from certain payer contracts due to aggressive hospital competition. Here, the challenge for the surgery center is showing the hospital provides more than simple competition, but rather has conspired to harm the physician-owned surgery center or has made an effort to monopolize the market. This can be a very expensive process of gathering facts to prove such conspiracy exists.

HIPAA: The Health Insurance Portability and Accountability Act (HIPAA) continues to be updated in a manner that adds additional burdens. One of the biggest burdens in the most recent HIPAA amendments requires a patient be notified of most inadvertent uses or disclosure of PHI (protected health information). Previously, centers and healthcare providers could decide, on a case-by-case basis, whether to notify the patient of a non-permitted use or disclosure. Now, patients must be notified of any use or disclosure were based on a four-factor test, the center cannot determine that there is a low risk that the PHI has been compromised. Further, under recent additions by the Health Information Technology for Economic and Clinical Health Act (HITECH), which has modified and strengthened the standards originally created by HIPAA, the patient has the right to receive copies of electronic medical records with little cost even if the surgery center must incur costs to provide the medical records.

These HIPAA and HITECH Act issues are as much of a concern for small providers like ASCs as they are for larger providers. Enforcement in general has been increasing since the additions of HITECH, with OCR reporting more than 133 million people have been affected by 1,221 HITECH Act related breaches through May 17, 2015.

This also should concern ASCs as enforcement actions have proceeded against smaller covered entities as well as larger ones. For example, OCR settled with Adult & Pediatric Dermatology PC, a private practice delivering dermatology services in four locations in Massachusetts and two in New Hampshire. When approximately 2,200 individuals had PHI on a laptop stolen from a vehicle of a staff member, the then OCR director Leon Rodriguez stated "That is what a good risk management process is all about – identifying and mitigating the risk before a bad thing happens. Covered entities of all sizes need to give priority to securing electronic protected health information."

The HITECH Act also mandated a random audit program, initiated by the OCR in 2011, requiring HHS to perform periodic audits of covered entity and business associate compliance with HIPAA privacy, security and breach notification rules. OCR established a comprehensive audit protocol organized around modules, representing separate elements of privacy, security and breach notification. The combination of these multiple requirements may vary based on the type of covered entity selected for review, with ASCs included in the providers to be audited. The audit program has been on hold since the conclusion of the pilot audit program and we anticipate the full program starting later this year.

Patient Disclosure

New conditions of coverage require an ASC patient be notified of certain information related to physician ownership and related to advance directives. The disclosure must be in writing and prior to the procedure. This requirement will make it critical that physicians become more engaged in the process of physician disclosure. The surgery center must take steps to assure it is comfortable that disclosure is happening at the proper time. The requirement includes the interpretive guidelines which state: "An ASC that has physician owners or investors must provide written notice to the patient, the patient's representative or surrogate, prior to the start of the surgical procedure, that the ASC has physician-owners or physicians with a financial interest in the ASC."

The new language regarding advance directives states:

The ASC must comply with the following requirements: (i) Provide the patient or, as appropriate, the patient's representative with written information concerning its policies on advance directives, including a description of applicable state health and safety laws and, if requested, official state advance directive forms. (ii) Inform the patient or, as appropriate, the patient's representative of the patient's right to make informed decisions regarding the patient's care. (iii) document in a prominent part of the patient's current medical record, whether or not the individual has executed an advance directive. 42 C.F.R. § 416.50(c) (2015)

HealthCare Reform

No one knows exactly what the ultimate impact of healthcare reform will be on ASCs. However, almost everyone expects it will lead to an incremental increase in the number of governmental and lower paying patients. In the short run, health care reform does not appear to have a very immediate negative impact on surgery centers. In fact, because the statute provides certain incentives for preventive efforts, such as colonoscopies, and because there is no public option, there may be some positive aspects for certain ASCs. However, health care reform does seem to be leading to increased consolidation of health systems and a reduction in independent physicians.

Certain of the concepts set forth in the health care reform law involve integrative efforts between hospitals and physicians to develop accountable care organizations and other efforts that allow the joint packaging of care. These efforts, together with other payment incentives for hospitals often lead to more employment of physicians by hospitals. This reduction in the pool of physicians means a reduction in the lifeblood of surgery centers.

While the overall verdict on health care reform is not yet in, certain of the long-term trends do not favor ambulatory surgical centers despite the fact that ASCs can reduce the cost of care.

Appendix IV
Recommended Reading

The Richest Man in Babylon by George Clason – perhaps the best book ever on personal finance. This is told in a parable format and is a short, easy to read gem.

How to Win Friends and Influence People by Dale Carnegie – published in 1937 and still as relevant as ever. The best book on social interaction and developing social skills.

The Little Book of Common Sense Investing by John Bogle – the power of low cost, index fund investing from the founder of Vanguard.

Rich Dad, Poor Dad by Robert Kiyosaki – entrepreneurship and how to create passive income. His follow up book, Cash Flow Quadrant is also highly recommended.

The Millionaire Next Door by Thomas Stanley – a sociologist's study of high-income earners and the wealthy. Insight into the habits of the wealthy, how they accumulate wealth and how they distinguish themselves from high income under accumulators of wealth.

Appendix IV

A Random Walk Down Wall Street by Burton Malkiel – originally published in 1973 and now in its 8th edition, this classic is an examination of the efficient market hypothesis written by a Princeton economics professor who argues that professional money managers cannot predict stock movements any better than someone predicting what path a drunk man in a field will take, hence the term random walk. Put another way, short-term price moves are unpredictable so paying professionals for their skill picking investments is likely a loser's game.

Appendix V
Summary of the Core Concepts

CONCEPT 1: *How you deal with people (Patients, Colleagues, Staff, Spouse, Family) will have more to do with your long-term success than your medical skills.* You must have both, but there are thousands who are just as smart, and have the essential skills. Note that nothing about billing or finances was just discussed because they are the secondary lessons. Acquiring emotional intelligence and effectively interacting/connecting with people are the initial building blocks to success in business.

CONCEPT 2: You must completely understand all aspects of your employment or partnership arrangement before you commit. In summary, who are you working with and what are the terms of your engagement with the group and expectations from the group?

CONCEPT 3: The critical lesson is to *negotiate your compensation* using benchmarks and it is recommended to use a qualified advisor to negotiate on your behalf. Taking the first offer is leaving money on the table in most instances, so be a smart negotiator because you will be working hard and should be paid accordingly and equitably.

CONCEPT 4: Before you buy into a practice, make sure that you understand the key terms of your partnership agreement, have a solid assessment of the fiscal health of the practice and use objective data to ensure that you pay fair market value for the practice.

CONCEPT 5: Coding compliance is a serious topic and one of the most common ways that physicians get into trouble. Use a third-party coding company as a protection against this and follow their recommendations unless you strongly disagree with them. In that instance, obtain another coding audit to act as the decider. Making a concerted effort to be compliant is essential.

CONCEPT 6: What gets measured, gets done. A monthly, quarterly, and yearly review of benchmarks and financial statements to identify areas of improvement or anomalies is a fundamental and essential strategy for running your practice and alerts your internal team that the practice efficiency is a priority.

CONCEPT 7: Your collections are your fiscal lifeline so ensuring that sound processes are in place and those processes are working is essential. Maintaining those systems using your accountant, practice manager and business advisor is a crucial part of being a successful practicing physician.

CONCEPT 8: Build your Tribe of advisors to protect your interests and remember that alignment of incentives is the key, particularly with your Tribe. Maintain a system of checks and balances with your Tribe, but this is a relationship (as will most things) and paying your advisors fairly and having them working with you for a common goal, mitigates problems for you in the future. Your Tribe protects you so choose good ones, stay close with them, and bond with them.

CONCEPT 9: The building block of acquiring wealth is being a committed investor and investing by growing your balance sheet and accelerating the power of compounding. Pay Yourself First and invest smartly every month without exception. The price of success if high, but so are the rewards.

CONCEPT 10:   Buy assets, not liabilities.

CONCEPT 11:   The key to being wealthy is very simple, yet sometimes hard to grasp: 1) don't spend everything you make - Pay Yourself First by automatically investing 10% to 20% of your after tax income, 2) commit to investing for the long-run in low cost investments that diversify your portfolio such as an index mutual funds tracking the S&P 500, Wilshire 5000 and the bond market, 3) control and limit your debt, 4) be rationale, turn off CNBC and understand that fluctuations in the market are normal, 5) play the long game, stay the course with your consistent investment plan and let the "magic" of compound interest work for you

CONCEPT 12: Personal finance can be summarized as follows:

- Buy assets not liabilities. Assets are items that appreciate, and liabilities depreciate.

- Your goal is to be wealthy or balance sheet rich holding assets that appreciate and generate passive income. Earning a high income is good but it means nothing if you have no cattle.

- To become wealthy, commit to your Investment Plan: "Pay Yourself First" - put 10% to 20% of your tax home pay in low cost, indexed mutual funds tracking major market indexes each month.

- Be a committed investor by automatically debiting your investment each month so you won't be tempted to forego your Investment Plan.

- Playing good defense is critical and this means controlling your expenses so you can follow your investment plan.

- Debt is the anchor to building wealth. Pay off your bad debt and only maintain debt that is used to augment your net worth.

- Developing an insurance strategy is very important. It is your key risk management tool.

- Understand that taxes are your biggest expense and understand how they work. Tax avoidance is illegal, tax deferment within the law is smart.

- Use estate planning tools to provide for your loved ones. Have a will, a living will (advanced directives) and a power of attorney.

- Use revocable trusts and irrevocable trusts to your advantage.

CONCEPT 13: Think of the market like a sports car. You don't want to redline it all the time, the engine needs a break so it can perform and finish the race so welcome market corrections and bubbles. They will occur with regularity so don't be surprised by them. The market corrects itself over the long run and true value is recognized. Avoid the siren song of bubbles and diversify your portfolio, stay the course, and stick with your investment plan.

CONCEPT 14: Professionally managed portfolios over the long run have not beaten their benchmarked indexes over the course of several studies. In addition, after factoring in cost, the data strongly correlates with efficient market theory – markets are efficient and hence professionals are at no more of an advantage than amateurs (or monkeys).

CONCEPT 15: Diversify - Don't put all your eggs in one basket.

CONCEPT 16: Time & Compounded Interest are your friend – be a Committed Investor

CONCEPT 17: Water finds its own level – over a period of time, stocks will offer higher returns than bonds because risk and return are linked. If stocks do not return more than bonds, investors will move money to safer investments (bonds) and the cash outflow will, in turn, lower the price of stocks which will then make them cheap enough to offer the type of return that will bring back investors. Thus, the market finds its own level balancing risk and return with higher expected returns favoring the riskier investments.